DUNK

David Boyle has been writing about new ideas for more than a quarter of a century. He is co-director of the New Weather Institute, a fellow of the New Economics Foundation, has stood for Parliament and is a former independent reviewer for the Cabinet Office. He is the author of *Alan Turing, Scandal* and *Before Enigma,* as well as a range of other historical studies.
He lives in the South Downs.

DUNKIRK
A miracle of
deliverance

David Boyle

THE REAL PRESS
www.therealpress.co.uk

Published in 2017 by the Real Press.
www.therealpress.co.uk © David Boyle
Kindle edition published by Endeavour Press

ISBN 978-1547045365

To Christopher,
With love.

"He then refloated her. He had no crew, save one stoker, but he gathered a British NCO and eight soldiers and with these put off for England."
John Masefield, *Nine Days Wonder* (1941), describing the Dunkirk voyage of the motor yacht, Maid Errant.

"We sailed when the last man was off, an' there were more than seven hunder' of us haboard a boat built to take two hunder'. 'E was still there when we left, an' 'e waved us good-bye and sails off towards Dunkirk, and the bird wiv' im. Blimey it was queer to see the ruddy big goose flyin' around 'is boat, lit up by the fires like a white hangel against the smoke."
Paul Gallico, *The Snow Goose* (1940)

Contents

Introduction   5

Sunday 19 May   17
Monday 20 May   24
Tuesday 21 May   28
Wednesday 22 May   31
Thursday 23 May   35
Friday 24 May   39
Saturday 25 May   44
Sunday 26 May   49
Monday 27 May   58
Tuesday 28 May   70
Wednesday 29 May   78
Thursday 30 May   90
Friday 31 May   97
Saturday 1 June   105
Sunday 2 June   110
Monday 3 June   115

Aftermath   118

Introduction

Three quarters of a century on from the disaster of Dunkirk, you can still see the places where the drama was played out – the evacuation of a whole army from the harbour and beaches. The harbour is tidy now and it is hard to imagine it filled with bodies and sunken ships, or the smoke from burning oil that so dominated the scene in May and June 1940. The long sandy beaches where the soldiers queued under the waves of attacking dive-bombers for days and nights now looks peaceful and sumptuous in the summer sunshine, as you would expect from France's most northerly seaside resort.

In England, you can still see the warren of Napoleonic era tunnels under Dover Castle, 26 metres below ground inside the White Cliffs, where the evacuation was planned and controlled, within the limitations of very difficult communications with the ships off the French and Belgian coasts. You can descend under the battered sign which says 'Vice-Admiral, Dover' deep into the rock to the set of tunnels known as Casemate Z, where Vice-Admiral Bertram Ramsay managed the so-called 'miracle', and where his small team of men and women worked, ate and slept at the height of the battle.

None of these quiet, peaceful places now betray the fact that, for nine days that summer, they were the backdrop for an extraordinary series of events that decided the fate of nations, and was to form part of the founding myth of the modern British state.

What you won't get to see is the cave hewn out of the rock, which provided office and sleeping quarters for Ramsay himself, and provided him with a balcony overlooking Dover Harbour, and from where – on clear nights – he could see the burning ports of Calais and Dunkirk.

This is a little peculiar, given the importance of Ramsay's 'Igloo', as he called it, but it is – or so you will be told by English Heritage – used to keep old computer equipment in. And somehow this is symbolic. Because we all know the myth of Dunkirk, the little ships and the miracle escape, but the story is rarely told in its full context and, perhaps, rarely in its *full* horror, with the blood carefully excised. The heart of the story is rarely told, but it is only when you get to the heart of it that we can see more clearly how Dunkirk was such a turning point for the British, and for

Europe – and how it came so much to symbolise the moment of change that we live with even today.

That is what this short book tries to do, to tell the whole story and, as far as possible, from the point of view of those, like Ramsay, at the heart of it. Because, every forty years or so, the economic and political assumptions by which the UK is governed get overturned. But they were never overturned quite so fast – never has disaster loomed so quickly and been averted with such speed – as it was during the end of May and the beginning of June 1940. As a result, from this very room deep inside the cliffs, under the presiding genius of Bertram Ramsay, a broken Britain which realised too late how they had been misled by their leaders, was miraculously forged anew.

The fact that the rescue was able to happen at all, not without loss and tragedy – and not without a betrayal of Britain's European allies – was certainly nothing short of miraculous. And we can look back on those few days in summer as the very moment that the nation we live in now was shaped.

Bertram Home Ramsay was born in 1883 and became, by accident, an early specialist in amphibious operations, commanding his first landing on a hostile beach on East Indies Station before the First World War, when he was a sub-lieutenant.

He also became known for his staggering stubbornness. What he lacked in stature, he made up for in determination. He would not accept defeat. This was an advantage in wartime but not necessarily when the navy was at peace.

He spent most of the First World War as part of the elite Dover Patrol, first commanding a monitor and then in command of the famous destroyer *Broke*. He took part with vigour and courage in the Second Ostend Raid, the failed attempt to block the harbour, where he was considered to have acquitted himself with honour.

In peacetime, he rose rapidly and was respected as a doyen of efficiency, and was also known as something of a martinet, though he had more than a human side too. He was destined for the very top of the peacetime navy but, as so often in the forces in those days, his relationship with one commanding officer undermined his career. This was Admiral Sir Roger Backhouse, who was appointed as Commander-in-Chief of the Home

Fleet in 1934 with Ramsay as his chief of staff. Backhouse was not a man given to delegation and Ramsay became increasingly frustrated in his role. Something happened in 1937 and he stepped down and went on half pay back to his home in Scotland. He turned down a job in China and found himself on the Retired List.

Backhouse went on to become head of the navy as First Sea Lord, and died of a brain tumour just before the outbreak of war. It had been a period of intense deference in the armed forces in the UK, starved of cash and investment, and also as a result starved of new ideas. This was so in the army in particular, which was still wedded to pre-war parade ground ideas, and had not yet learned the lessons of armoured warfare that the British had taught the world so unexpectedly at the battle of Cambrai in 1917. But it was also to some extent true of the navy, which had struggled to survive the various arms limitation treaties and a full scale mutiny over pay at Invergordon in 1931.

Although they did not know it at the time, the Royal Navy was so complacent about its ability to crack codes that it was unaware that its own naval codes were being read every day by the German navy, and had been since 1936.

What brought Ramsay back from retirement in

the Scottish borders was the war scare in September 1938, when the nation came so close to going to war over Czechoslovakia. In the week of what became the Munich Crisis, the navy awoke to the fact that war was imminent and they had not really prepared for it. They searched their lists, including the Retired List, for any officers with the right expertise. Ramsay was known as an effective leader and had made his name as part of the Dover Patrol in the First World War, and the Admiralty needed a flag officer to take charge of the front line port of Dover who was capable of blocking the English Channel to enemy shipping and submarines.

Delighted to be back, Ramsay found himself appointed as Vice-Admiral, Dover and – two days before Prime Minister Neville Chamberlain met Hitler, Mussolini and the French premier Edouard Daladier in Munich – he arrived in Kent with a small staff, some of whom had found themselves in the job before they could actually buy a uniform.

"Before leaving Chatham, I was fortunate in obtaining a small supply of stationery from the commander-in-chief's office," Ramsay complained. "But apart from this, I had no typewriter, books, forms or any of the customary appurtenances of a captain's office, let alone an admiral's office."

There were no headquarters available. Dover Castle, the medieval pile on the cliffs, was hardly suitable. The harbourmaster's office, where he could have used the boardroom, closed at 5pm every night. To start with, his staff took calls in Brown's Hotel, where they were staying. One of them borrowed a wireless set from Chatham Dockyard and set it up in the castle. It had a range of only 60 miles – not enough to reach the Commander-in-Chief at Chatham. When they used the ordinary phone lines, it took an hour to get through. It was quicker to send a despatch rider. There should have been a wireless station at the docks. There had been one, but it had been converted into a public toilet.

"The feeling of being, during a time of emergency, deaf and dumb as regards communications, of being homeless as regards places in which to establish a command is one which I hope not to have to experience again," he wrote.

The harbour also needed dredging. Ramsay soon came up with proposals, including closing the western entrance to the harbour and building an oil depot inside the East Cliff. He was going to be allocated 18 destroyers, 49 converted trawlers and other auxiliary vessels, two minelayers two minesweepers, plus five other escort ships.

With these tools his task was to close the English Channel to the enemy, but also to transport and supply the British Expeditionary Force, known henceforth by the acronym BEF, which would be sent to support the French and Belgians in the event of a war with Nazi Germany. It was a tall order. "We have no stationary, books, typists or machines, no chairs, and few tables, maddening communications," Ramsay wrote home to his wife, Margaret. "I pray that war, if it has to come, will be averted for a few days."

But Ramsay's prayers were answered. As it turned out, the Munich meeting ended in a controversial agreement which allowed Hitler to take the Sudetenland, the largely German speaking region of Czechoslovakia. There was "peace in our time", Chamberlain told the crowds as that welcomed him home at Croydon Airport. So Ramsay and his small staff were stood down again.

Ramsay went back to Margaret – Mags, he called her. Dover harbour was dredged in case of war and many of his other suggestions were taken in hand. The nation was waking up to the danger, but had yet to realise quite how unprepared they were. But when, nearly six months later, in March 1939, Hitler broke the agreement and marched into the rest of Czechoslovakia, and began to threaten Poland, war became inevitable and Ramsay was recalled for a second time. This time, he found he was expected to perform the same duties with only seven destroyers, four minelayers, and a handful of other ships, including two converted ferries.

Still, like everyone else, the slow pace of the war when it came – even at sea – took them all by surprise in the early days, when it was known as the 'Phoney War', and Ramsay was in town shopping for sherry to take home to his wife. "At least we have the summer to look forward to," he wrote.

The early months of the war, Ramsay's main problem had been the new German magnetic mines, which caused terrible damage during the winter until courageous bomb disposal teams began to work out techniques for dealing with them. Then, in April 1940, Hitler invaded Norway and everything changed. Most of Ramsay's ships were withdrawn from his command, leaving only five working corvettes and seven motor torpedo boats (MTBs). The allied failures in Norway also led to a political crisis which toppled Chamberlain from power on the day that Hitler launched his offensive in the West. When Winston Churchill became prime minister, at this crucial moment in the nation's history, he feared the worst. "I hope it's not too late," he said to his bodyguard after seeing the King. "I very much fear that it is."

Ramsay had been at the heart of operational planning since that day, 10 May, because he was responsible for keeping Lord Gort, the BEF's commander-in-chief, and his men supplied in Belgium. Three days before the offensive, when it was apparent what was about to happen, he had been ordered to be ready to send ships to Antwerp, Flushing, Ijmuiden and the Hook of Holland, to fetch out Dutch shipping and destroy the oil supplies.

In the event, Dutch forces were able to hold off the Nazi advance for only three days and Ramsay despatched two cruisers, *Arethusa* and *Galatea* to fetch the Dutch gold reserves, and some of his remaining destroyers to collect the Dutch royal family, after a direct phone call for help from Queen Wilhelmina to George VI. He also sent a landing party to collect as many diamonds from the vaults of Amsterdam as possible. It had been a successful operation.

The collapse of the French will to fight over the next few weeks was a terrible shock to everyone on both sides of the Channel. It is possible to say now that the British decision to withdraw their forces to Dunkirk may have contributed to this, but this was more of a symptom than a cause. The French had been assumed to have the most powerful army in Europe, and it was highly regarded. But neither the British nor the French military authorities had grasped how much war had changed over the previous generation, just how mobile and how terrifying it could be – when all the Nazis needed to burst through resistance to a fast tank advance was to call in the Stuka dive bombers. Neither the British nor the French had the right technology, or the right planes, to tackle mechanical warfare on that scale.

Unlike the other two services, the navy had been tested since the outbreak of war, and they had been building modern destroyers for the past four years as fast as they could. It was a long way from being enough, but they were comparatively confident in their technology – though, like the RAF's shortage of experienced pilots, there was a worrying shortage of trained and effective destroyer commanders.

By now Ramsay and his small staff were in a

series of caves carved out of the cliff below Dover Castle and whitewashed. Ramsay called it his 'Igloo'. Next door to his office was the operations room, with a large wooden table which tracked the ship movements in the sector of sea that Ramsay was responsible for – between those under the control of commands in the Nore, protecting the Thames Estuary and the east coast and Portsmouth.

From there, he was about to preside over the most extraordinary crisis, which brought together all the failures of the past – and required his fortitude to rescue the nation in just nine days. It was to be a huge achievement, in moral rather than physical courage, in endurance and leadership, but above all in innovative and inspired organisation.

Sunday 19 May

The French government ministers trooped off to Notre Dame Cathedral in Paris, an unprecedented religious gesture for a nation which had an anti-clerical constitution. Because it was a Sunday, Churchill was relaxing for the first time since taking office at home at Chartwell in Kent. A rumour had reached the War Office that the French First Army, all that lay between the BEF and the advancing bulk of the German invaders, had disappeared. Gort and his staff were trying to make contact with them, but where were they?

They already knew that the BEF was squeezed between the German advance through Belgium and the Netherlands and the accelerating advance by their armoured columns, led up through the Ardennes and to the Channel by the tank pioneer Heinz Guderian. But this was new.

Should War Office officials tell the prime minister? Churchill was summoned to the phone in Kent and ordered a police escort back to London. An hour or so later, at 10 Downing Street, he put a phone call through directly to Gort's headquarters at Habarcq, a small village eight miles west of Arras. Where was the French army? Had they really disappeared?

Gort was out but his chief of staff Henry Pownall took the call, and he reassured Churchill that the reports were exaggerated. But the truth was that Pownall and Gort were also very concerned about their allies. At midnight the night before, they had gone through an unnerving meeting with the French commander-in-chief Gaston Billotte, commander of the northern armies and their own direct senior officer. Billotte had arrived looking ashen and exhausted. "I am completely tired and I can't do a thing about these panzers," he told them.

The French command was in disarray because the head of the army, Maurice Gamelin, had just been sacked and Maxine Weygand recalled from North Africa to replace him. Billotte told Gort he had no reserves to call up.

It had been a worrying meeting. "My God," said Pownall, after he had gone. "How awful to be allied to so temperamental a race." So Pownall now told Churchill that Gort was thinking of falling back to the Channel ports, if he still had time. But as he weighed his remaining options, Gort was aware that he had to contemplate an order from Billotte to withdraw south instead, to the River Senne, aware that this would mean there would then be no chance to escape to the Channel if necessary. "I am not prepared to lose my force," Gort told Pownall.

So what could the BEF do? At six that morning, Gort and his closest staff had discussed their options: counterattacking to the south east into Belgium, counterattacking towards Arras to the south west or running for the coast. The trouble was that the first two options could only be effective if they could rely on the French to coincide with them and, if Billotte's exhaustion was widespread, this seemed unlikely. All day and all night, Lieutenant-Colonel Lord Bridgeman, keeping himself awake with chocolate and whisky, devised a plan for an ordered withdrawal to the sea.

Back in England, Ramsay made the journey up to London for a meeting at the War Office about the increasingly beleaguered position of the BEF. It was significant that the navy had been invited at all, largely because of the question of how to keep Lord Gort supplied across the Channel – and what to do if that became impossible.

The fighting had now moved to the coast as the Belgian army began to fall back under pressure from German air raids. Ramsay's ships were now fighting there alongside the French vessels, which were able to refuel in desperation only from petrol pumps near the docks. It was there today that two of Ramsay's scarce, though oldest, destroyers were sunk by dive bombers. Both *Valentine* and *Whitley* went down off the Belgian coast. It was a worrying sign of how badly prepared the British ships were against aircraft attack – which was to become horribly clear in the first two years of the war.

The meeting at the War Office was organised to discuss whether the BEF was in real danger, because it was suddenly clear that the German advance though Belgium threatened to cut Gort off from the Channel ports through which he got his supplies – and through which he might need to escape if the advance carried on at its current speed.

Could you evacuate the BEF, Ramsay was asked? It seemed unlikely at the time that anywhere near enough of them could be taken off. The meeting agreed that, if any kind of evacuation was to happen, Ramsay would be in charge. He went back to his Igloo and warned his staff about the possibility, but told them it was unlikely to happen.

In the war cabinet meeting at 10 Downing

Street that day, Churchill himself was thinking along similar lines. He raised the idea of gathering small ships in ports in the south of England ready to send over quickly if the BEF was stranded for whatever reason on the coast. Vice Admiral Sir Lionel Preston at the Admiralty formed the Small Ships Pool, of 43 boats gathered at Westminster Pier – but more would be needed.

Because of that, just days after taking office as prime minister, Churchill was preparing for the ultimate emergency – the potential loss of most of the British army. The War Minister Anthony Eden had already announced the formation of the Home Guard, and asked able-bodied men to come forward. A huge number did so. Later that same evening (14 May), the BBC had broadcast this announcement:

"The Admiralty have made an order directing the owners of self-propelled pleasure craft between thirty and one hundred feet in length to send all particulars to the Admiralty within fourteen days from today, if they have not already been offered or requisitioned."

By this day, five days later, retired Rear Admiral Alfred Taylor had been given powers to collect and pay crews of small craft which might be used by navy, and was gathering them at

Sheerness in the Thames estuary. The man in charge of finding the ships, H. C. Riggs, was now sleeping at the offices of the Ministry of Shipping in Berkeley Square, one of the administrative heroes of Dunkirk, and was collecting information on small ships that might be available and holding them in port. The clerks at the Admiralty were printing copies of form T124, which signed people up for 90 days short service in the navy.

Gort was also taking an interim decision. He decided to send his headquarters staff, anyone who could be spared, including his intelligence officers, back to Dunkirk by special train, to get them out of the way. There had been for some days a tacit understanding that the brightest British army officers should be sent home just in case. By the official start of Operation Dynamo on 26 May, as many as 28,000 soldiers had already been collected from Dunkirk harbour.

Gort's other decision was to send Colonel Hewer back to London to discuss how in practice the whole of the BEF might be evacuated from the same place.

Then there was the crisis in the RAF. Just as the army had neglected to think ahead about modern technology or tactics, so the RAF was finding itself outclassed in the air. Their Fairey

Battle fighter-bombers made occasional, desperate bombing forays had left only a handful of planes still airworthy and only a few pilots still alive in Belgium. The RAF commander attached to the BEF had sat sobbing with his head in his hands.

The dilemma was all the more intense for Churchill, who was determined to persuade the French that the British were good allies, when the French premier Paul Reynaud had requested ten more British squadrons to be sent to France.

Sir Hugh Dowding at Fighter Vommand was a shy and mystical person – he believed in fairies and other less predictable personality traits in high military command – but he protested in the strongest terms. "We have to face the fact that they may be defeated," he told the war cabinet in a desperate memo. There came a point when they had to conserve their forces for the defence of Britain. On 16 May, he had been summoned to the war cabinet and, to his surprise, found that they backed him. The squadrons of precious Spitfires and Hurricanes were not sent.

Monday 20 May

This was the day it became clear just how much danger the BEF was now in, not so much because of the German advance through Belgium, which was worrying enough, but because of the advance of Guderian's panzer divisions through Sedan. Guderian had moved so fast that he was now rapidly approaching Boulogne. Boulogne and Calais had been the ports designated to supply the BEF, and the War Office had estimated that British forces on the continent would need 200 tons of stores a day if they were to be cut off from their supply lines in France. To do that, as a bare minimum, they would need to supply through both Boulogne and Calais.

In the morning, Gort's emissary Colonel Hewer arrived at the War Office to find that the Chief of the Imperial General Staff (CIGS), Sir Edmund Ironside, the head of the army, had gone to France. Ironside spoke seven languages – he is said to have been the model for John Buchan's hero Richard Hannay – and had close links with the French army. It was one of the reasons he was in a job he didn't enjoy (he had wanted Gort's job), and he was appalled at the idea of withdrawal. Churchill had urged him to go immediately to clarify matters to Gort, and to order him to attack to the south west the following day, to link up with French forces.

Ironside and Pownall then went to see Billotte together and found him depressed – "No plan, no thought of a plan," wrote Ironside later. "Ready to be slaughtered." Ironside, a huge man, lost his temper and shook Billotte by his tunic buttons, insisting that they attack Cambrai together the next day.

Gort claimed that he had no orders from the French for some days. This was not entirely true. The British were going through one of those tortuous changes of policy which required them to believe two contradictory things at the same time – that they were ignoring French orders and preparing to withdraw, while at the same time they were wholeheartedly committed to the Anglo-French alliance. People like Ironside, who had made the alliance possible, were in a particularly agonising position.

In Dover, Ramsay was beginning to think seriously about how an evacuation might be managed. He held a meeting in his Igloo with army officials and on the agenda was an item for discussion called "emergency evacuation across the Channel of very large

forces". The full implications were not spelled out, but they were clear to everyone in the room what was actually being discussed – and the consequences of failure.

Immediately after the meeting, Ramsay's staff and their colleagues in the Admiralty and Ministry of Shipping in London began compiling lists of the ships which they would call on at short notice. These were mainly ferries – mostly the paddle steamers which had operated out of Portsmouth across the Solent or from Dover across the Channel, some of which were already used for naval duties. The Isle of Man ferries were also available.

Someone at the Admiralty mentioned that the Dutch barges known as *schuyts*, which had flat bottoms and crews of three, might be very suitable for taking people off beaches. As many as forty of them had arrived in the previous weeks from the Netherlands and were in the Thames estuary. Ramsay gave orders to have them requisitioned and manned by crews from the naval reserve.

He also took what turned out to be a critical decision. He ordered 80,000 cans of drinking water and sent them to Dunkirk to special dumps, and set guards on them. It turned out to have a vital significance in keeping the army alive.

Tuesday 21 May

Dawn marked the start of the British counterattack, designed to threaten the German supply lines and cut off the advancing panzers from the safety of the rest of their army. The agreement with the French stipulated that the British would attack south of Arras and towards Cambrai. Their attacks would be timed to coincide.

Major-General Harold Franklyn, in command of the action, had been expecting the arrival of a French liaison officer. But the time was getting on and he decided to go ahead anyway, and with the only tanks available to him, just sixteen of them. With an hour to go, a message came through that the French had decided to postpone for the following day. Unsure if he had the time to recall his forces, Franklyn let the attack begin. It was a crucial decision which guaranteed the failure of the alliance but paradoxically, as it turned out, the success of the evacuation.

To make matters worse, the British sighted French tanks, thought they were German and attacked them. The German commander charged with the task of resisting was a man who would soon be the most famous German general of them all, then known as Major-General Erwin Rommel. By 6pm, Rommel had prevailed, the attack was over and the remaining British tanks – and most of the commanders had been killed – were in retreat. At one stage they were reduced to putting dinner plates upside down on the road, waiting for the German tank columns to stop and investigate, then leaping out and attacking their crews.

But despite the failure of the British offensive, the German high command had been rattled. Just for a moment, they feared the worst – that their tanks would be cut off. It was to lead to a crucial decision to halt – which in the end was enough to save the BEF and therefore the British ability to fight at all. "A critical moment on the drive came as my forces reached the Channel," said General Gerd von Rundstedt later, one of the three main commanders of the invasion force. "For a short time, we feared that our armoured divisions could be cut off before the infantry divisions could come up and support them."

Now that his offensive had clearly failed, and there had been no sign of the French offensive that was supposed to have taken place alongside theirs, it seemed likely to Gort that he had no option but to race for the Channel ports. On the other hand, he had been ordered otherwise, not just by his French senior commander but by Churchill himself, who was desperate not to give the French the impression of any excuse to renege on their own commitments to the alliance. But he waited. The fate of the BEF hung in the balance.

Wednesday 22 May

The plight of the port of Boulogne emphasised the great dilemma which the British were now in. Should they reinforce or should they run? If they were to reinforce and fail, then it would make it even harder to escape. But if they were to cut and run, it would abandon their French allies to their fate. The same question was rising up the agenda of the war cabinet, not just over the French request for more squadrons or the fate of the BEF, but whether to defend or abandon Boulogne.

In this case, Ramsay and the army decided to keep their options open. They sent demolition parties to Boulogne, but they also sent reinforcements in the form of two battalions, of the Welsh and Irish Guards, both of which were sent down early in the day from their barracks at Camberley in Surrey, and found themselves fighting by the evening. Boulogne's French commander had in fact already ordered an evacuation – for which he was sentenced after the war to twenty years in prison – but the French marines fought brilliantly and were still holding on.

The Guards landed to find a chaotic situation in the town, as large numbers of British and French troops wandered round, many of them drunk. The Guards fought to take control, but Ramsay's destroyers – which had brought them over and were now sheltering in the harbour – were being shelled by German troops in the outskirts of the town.

"Personally, I think we cannot extricate the British Expeditionary Force," Ironside confided in his diary. "Only hope a march south west. Have they time? Have they the food? God help the BEF, brought to this state by the incompetence of the French command."

Meanwhile, in London and Dover, Ramsey's preparations were accelerating. If he was going to send hundreds of small ships across the Channel, he would need charts. Where would they come from at short notice? He was able to requisition many of them from Stanford's map shop in London's Long Acre, and then there was a stroke of luck. Admiralty staff remembered that the *Daily Telegraph* had given away a detailed map of the Channel free to readers some weeks before: did they have any stocks left over? A phone call to Fleet Street was enough to secure them. Then they had to be distributed to Dover, Ramsgate and

Sheerness. But first, Ramsay had to designate the safest routes, avoiding obvious minefields, and recommending them to take a route directly over the Channel and then along the coast to Dunkirk, aware that this might become impossible depending on how far the German guns had managed to advance. By the end, Admiralty staff managed to find over a thousand charts and they marked the routes on half of them, aware that – in some cases – they would be only of limited use. Small boats designed to meander up and down the Thames were not often equipped with navigation equipment.

Mass Observation, the pioneering opinion testing organisation, found that people were remarkably optimistic, not to say ignorant, about the plight of the BEF. There appeared to be a sharp class division, with working class men the most optimistic and middle class women the least. Harold Nicholson, now a junior information minister, wrote his diary in Sissinghurst Castle that evening: "I look around the garden feeling I may never see it again." But he was an insider; he knew some of the truth.

Despite the optimism, time was running out. That night, Ramsay could sit at his desk in the Igloo and see the glow of the fires as the Second

Panzer Division and the Guards battalions fought it out around the docks of Boulogne, just across the Channel.

Thursday 23 May

As dawn broke on the shattered dockside of
Boulogne, it was clear that there was no way that
the small garrison could survive, even with the
Guards and French marines providing a backbone.
The order was given to withdraw and 4,000
British soldiers were taken off by destroyer later
that day. Ramsay sent the old destroyers *Venetia*
and *Vimy*, with 200 sailors, to cover the
evacuation and organise the harbour as they took
them off. It was a very close call, but the soldiers
were taken aboard and, by the evening, they were
speeding back across the Channel.

But the way it was done, with no liaison with
French allies, did not bode well. A mistake by the
gun crews on the destroyer *Whitshed*, firing over
the heads of the Guards at what they thought were
German positions outside the town, hit defending
French soldiers. They in turn shifted their guns
onto the British in retaliation. It was hardly a good
omen. Nor did the British give any notice to the
French garrison that they were about to leave.
Worse, they sank a blockship in the harbour
mouth, effectively sealing it against any kind of

rescue for the French.

The evacuation of Boulogne as the panzers rolled in threw the weight of attention onto the fate of Calais, the next port in the way of the advancing tanks, moving along the coast from west to east. If Dunkirk was going to be held to take off even part of the BEF, then Calais would have to be held for most of that time. Orders were given to the troops fighting there that it must be held to the last round of ammunition. It was a brutal decision.

In fact, Guderian had already swept past Calais on his way to Dunkirk, leaving the defenders surrounded. Then the unexpected happened. General Ewald von Kleist ordered him to stop at the line of the canal outside Dunkirk.

At first, Guderian could not understand it and he ignored the order, sending his armoured cars tentatively across the line down which Gort was planning to escape. But as he did so, a more explicit order came through and Guderian recalled his advance guard and complied. He protested but was told that he was stopping on Hitler's direct orders.

What had happened was that the German army had deep misgivings about the western offensive, afraid that success would go to Hitler's head, as indeed it did, and the failed British offensive had made them nervous. Hitler in particular was worried about whether his tanks would manage to get through the marshy ground to the west of Dunkirk. He was also nervous at the prospect of Gamelin's inevitable counterattack from the south east. But his senior military advisers were divided about what to do. There were angry meetings at Hitler's military OKH headquarters, the operational command of the army.

There is some evidence to suggest that Hitler was reluctant to destroy the British, believing that the British empire – like the Roman Catholic church – was one of the pillars which held up the world (his favourite film was *Lives of a Bengal Lancer*). The controversial stop order was to have enormous implications, preventing Guderian from winning the war that week – it could be said to have been Hitler's fatal strategic error.

But that might be to put too much emphasis on his logical thinking. It transpired later that he and his Luftwaffe chief, Herman Goering, had a phone conversation the same day. Goering suggested that the safest way forward was to let the Luftwaffe get the glory of destroying the British army from the air. This may have been the main motivation for the stop order: it was a safer option than risking the tanks in the notorious marshes. So when Guderian complained directly to Kleist, he was told: "Dunkirk is to be left to the Luftwaffe."

The halt order was sent uncoded and was picked up by the War Office in London by Major-General Arthur Percival, the man who was later to preside over the loss of Singapore. Its full significance was not recognised at the time. At the same time, more disastrous news was arriving in London: General Billotte, who Ironside had gripped by the tunic buttons, had been killed at this critical moment outside Ypres.

Friday 24 May

"The news that the bulk of the British forces defending Boulogne managed to withdraw," wrote Brigadier John Charteris in the *Manchester Guardian*, "will do little to allay the anxiety that the fall of the port must inevitably cause."

There was nervousness back home, but also delusion. The *Daily Herald*, the standard bearer of the left, carried an article by their war correspondent which claimed that "Britain and France are unbeaten. The main French armies, the main British armies, have not yet been seriously engaged."

That was not obvious at the time in the English Channel, where the British destroyer *Wessex* was bombed and sunk off Calais while the large French destroyer *Chacal* suffered the same fate off Boulogne. The scenes of apocalyptic drunkenness, with French and British soldiers wandering around town shooting anyone they suspected of being spies, that the Guards had encountered in Boulogne had also now shifted to Calais, cut off by land by Guderian's advance.

Meanwhile, the dilemma faced by the British

was now intense. If they were really going to evacuate, then some sort of approach would have to be made to the French – just as Churchill was bending over backwards to reassure them that the British were the staunchest and most reliable allies. He wanted to make sure there would be no excuse for them to seek a separate peace. Here most of the British histories are economical with the truth, just as the British authorities were at the time. They dared not come clean about their plans, yet there had to be discussion, which is why Ramsay found himself expected to persuade the French naval authorities while not being entirely clear about British plans. He invited the senior French admirals, Gabriel Auphan and Jean-Marie Abrial, based in Dunkirk, who was the senior French admiral covering the northern coast of France.

Ironically, a window of opportunity had now opened that might just make a withdrawal possible. In the morning, Hitler flew into Charlesville to meet Kleist and confirmed his controversial stop order, explaining that some of Guderian's forces must instead go south to attack the new French army positions there. Why not take the opportunity of destroying the British while it was possible, Kleist asked him?

"That may be so," Hitler replied. "But I did not want to send the tanks into the Flanders marshes – and the British won't come back in this war."

Now desperate to breathe some backbone into the French alliance, Churchill countermanded orders to evacuate Calais and ordered the Canadian regiment which had arrived at Southampton docks that morning to sail directly there. Churchill also sent Brigadier Claude Nicholson to take command of the defence of the port, if only as a way of holding Dunkirk for a little longer.

A bitter signal was sent by the War Office to the Calais garrison ahead of Nicholson's arrival: "No, repeat, no evacuation means that you must comply for the sake of allied solidarity". Churchill was livid when he saw it and demanded that senior officials find out who sent it. That very day, the government bowed to press pressure against fifth columnists and interned the fascist leader Sir Oswald Mosley and his wife Diana. Churchill was obsessed with what he called 'defeatism' at the heart of the establishment.

At the same time, Nicholson had arrived in the beleaguered city in time to receive a message from the German commander outside calling on him to surrender. "The answer is no," he replied. "It is the

British army's duty to fight as well as it is the Germans."

He also discovered that the Canadian regiment which had been diverted from Southampton Docks had been turned back again on their way to Calais after an intervention by the senior Canadian officer in France, Major-General Andrew McNaughton, who sent a message directly to the war cabinet protesting that it was unthinkable that his country's finest troops should be thrown away on a hopeless battle to defend Calais.

This defeat now seemed just a matter of time and Gort had still made no absolute decision, though the moment was clearly approaching when he would have to commit. But today was also a key moment in the preparation of the evacuation when the French admirals arrived in Dover and were escorted to see Ramsay and his staff in the Igloo. Three days had passed since Ramsay had been asked by the Admiralty to prepare for the possibility of evacuation. Ramsay and his French counterparts managed to reach an outline agreement about who should command what, and the French officers left saying that they would lock the papers away and hope they would never be needed.

But Ramsay had become well-known for

speaking uncomfortable truths and said that, on the contrary, he was putting it into immediate effect by evacuating base personnel. Uproar followed. Ramsay had taken the decision to start without reference to higher authority. In fact, his ability to take his own decisions and ignore higher authority was what made the evacuation the success it was.

"We've been through and are going through an indescribable time," he wrote to his wife afterwards. "Days and nights are all one and we are dealing with a situation as complex as it is unsavoury ... It's been my lot to operate the naval part of this and anything more difficult and unpleasing I've never been faced with. At this very moment, we are racked with anxiety about the situation in Calais. I can't tell you of it, or of the anxiety with which I am confronted; I can only say that the latter increase with each hour and we are helpless to retrieve the position ... I am optimistic that we shall pull through and win the war in the end. But admittedly I have no cause to say so."

Saturday 25 May

People woke in the morning to some difficult reading. As well as the fears about fifth columnists and German refugees that obsessed the nation – largely without foundation, as it turned out – there was some accurate and unnerving reporting from France. "The threat to this island grows nearer and nearer," said the *Daily Express*. "While the people of Britain wait anxiously for news of their soldiers over the Channel, they must prepare for the onslaught which may come upon their own soil."

Early in the morning, the new supreme French commander Weygand had confirmed General Georges Blanchard in command of the French First Army, now that Billotte was dead. But for two crucial days, the allied forces in the north had been given no firm command. Weygand then left for the French war cabinet meeting in Paris, and his message was blunt. "France has committed the immense mistake of waging a war without either the equipment or the necessary strategic objective," he told them. "She will probably have to pay a high price for this foolishness."

In response, and for the first time, the new member of the French war council – brought back from heroic retirement – Marshal Philippe Pétain, broached the subject of an armistice. It was precisely this conversation that Churchill had been prepared to sacrifice so many British lives to prevent the French from opening. Since March, the two nations had been committed to a solemn treaty forbidding each other to make a separate peace. Pétain had said what had previously been left unsaid – that there might come a time when that treaty would have to be ignored.

There was a solemn agreement with the British not to seek a separate peace, but neither Weygand nor Pétain believed they were bound by it. "I question whether there is complete reciprocity with the British," said Pétain. "Actually they have given only two divisions while eighty French divisions are still fighting."

Reynaud disagreed but promised to go to London the following day and ask what they would do if Paris was to fall to the Nazis. In fact, the main item under discussion at their war council that morning was actually not the plight of the allies in north west France, but the imminent threat that Mussolini would bring the Italians into the war

on Hitler's side, and were about the declare war

against the allies. What resources could France possible spare to defend their southern border? That was not clear.

While the French war cabinet was meeting, the British foreign Secretary Lord Halifax was making an approach himself, asking to see the Italian ambassador, Giuseppe Bastianini. When they met that afternoon, both men skirted the real issue – whether Italy would act as an intermediary if necessary to Hitler – and concentrated instead on hinting that Italy might play a role in a wider European settlement. This was an unofficial approach, but Halifax wanted to know that, if he pressed this idea in the cabinet, that he wouldn't be rebuffed by the Italians.

At Gort's headquarters outside Arras, the debate was going back and forth. Should they commit to battle or should they withdraw? It was an agonising decision, but by 6.30 that evening, Gort had made it – and without reference to higher authority and without liaising with either the French or Belgian armies which were depending on him. After the debacle of the combined allied counterattack on 21/22 May, Gort had concluded that his French allies were unravelling and he therefore had no choice but to disobey direct orders from his French commanders, and the implicit orders from London. He ordered the BEF to make all speed for Dunkirk, and he asked the commander of III Corps, Lieutenant-General Sir Ronald Adam, to make arrangements for a defensive line around the beaches. It was a critical and historic decision.

On the face of it, Gort was right. His decision to withdraw made the Dunkirk evacuation possible and meant that Britain could fight on, and that the war would eventually be won. But it relied on an extreme series of strokes of luck and good weather, and there is another view – because Gort's decision also destroyed Weygand's plan for an Anglo-French offensive. It virtually guaranteed the fall of France. It embedded the idea of Britain as an unreliable partner, Perfidious Albion. As C. S. Lewis once wrote, you can never know what *would* have happened. There is an alternative history which, with the same degree of luck, might also have cut Guderian's supply lines and pushed back the invaders. It seems unlikely, but then so – at the time – did the escape from Dunkirk.

The man in London with the most responsibility for relations with the French military was the War Minister, Anthony Eden. He told Gort that Churchill would talk to Reynaud and sound him out about a possible embarkation.

This was not wholly honest. As the British knew very well, the embarkation had actually already begun and would begin officially the following day when the BEF's advance guard arrived at the coast.

Eden was careful. "In the meantime," he wrote, "it is obvious you should not discuss the possibility of the move with the French or Belgians." Eden could not quite bring himself to use the term evacuation, even to his own army commander. The British were desperately trying to save themselves and convince the French of their reliability both at the same time, and – to some extent – they were also able to convince themselves that there was no contradiction between them. But their allies would know all too soon.

Churchill's final orders to Ironside that evening was to tell Nicholson to hold out until the end in Calais. The last thing he did before turning in for sleep was to shift Ironside from his post, at his own request, to take charge of the defence of the UK.

The Germans "seem youthful, fresh, inventive," wrote the novelist Virginia Woolf in her diary that night. "We plod behind."

Sunday 26 May

King George VI and Queen Wilhelmina of the Netherlands, carrying their gas masks, went to a special service in Westminster Abbey. Churchill also arrived, explaining that he could only stay for ten minutes. The government had, in their very English way, managed to avoid an official day of prayer, in case it smacked of desperation, but still knew that the churches around the nation could be relied on to pray pretty fervently.

"The English are loath to expose their feelings," wrote Churchill later, "but in my stall in the choir I could feel the pent up, passionate emotion, and also the fear of the congregation, not of death or wounds or material loss, but of defeat and the final ruin of Britain."

If anywhere in the nation was aware of the peril they were in, it was the Westminster community. If the rest of the country was reading their newspapers where the danger was not being spelled out, Westminster knew and feared the future.

Churchill and his ministers left in the middle of

the service to meet Reynaud and his delegation from Paris. He had already held a war cabinet meeting beforehand, when Halifax revealed his conversations with the Italians and made his first move – emphasising that the priority was "safeguarding the independence of our empire and if possible that of France".

Churchill was careful. He had been prime minister for less than two weeks and, if he provoked Halifax into resigning, it could be disastrous both for him and the nation. He simply replied that a German-dominated Europe would never provide peace or security. When he and Chamberlain rushed off to Westminster Abbey, he asked the war cabinet to meet again at 2pm – after a lunch with Reynaud, who he told that Britain would fight on (though that issue had not yet been decided). Reynaud said he feared he could be forced out when he refused to sign a separate peace.

Two departments in Whitehall, opposite each other across the road, where the lights had been burning all weekend, and whose officials were probably not in the abbey that morning, were fearing the worst. In the Admiralty and the War Office, they knew that the BEF had been streaming northwards all night, with their rearguard also withdrawing slowly towards the sea. The time was rapidly approaching to start the evacuation in earnest.

Ramsay had dubbed it Operation Dynamo, partly after the machine which hummed away in his cave providing him with electricity. But it was a well-chosen name, because somehow the nation would have to generate unprecedented energy if they were going to escape.

He could look down from the Igloo that morning at Dover Harbour, packed with former cross-Channel ferries, begged, borrowed and stolen from other departments and commands, and mainly manned by civilian crews. There were navy destroyers, cargo ships, minesweepers and MTBs, plus a shabbier collection of Dutch and Belgian coasters and British fishing boats, plus ammunition and stores ships tied up ready for unloading, and four powerful tugs, *Simla*, *Gondia*, *Roman* and *Lady Brassey* fussing around the harbour mouth, ready to guide the big ships on their way.

Operation Dynamo was given the go-ahead a few minutes before 7pm, though Ramsay had been anticipating the order for some hours. At 3pm, he sent the so-called 'personnel vessels' – the ferries – ready to arrive as soon as order came. The start of his orchestra of small boats which had gathered at Ramsgate was also sent over in waves designed to avoid bunching off the Dunkirk coast. It was too much of a risk to just queue up, given that this would make them a target for the dive-bombers. Still in Ramsgate Harbour were four small Belgian ferries, plus the drifters and the motor boats borrowed from the Contraband Control unit, which were also based there.

The first difficulty, after the huge and not entirely successful efforts of Admiralty officials to crew all the available ships, was that Ramsay's shortest route to Dunkirk was now impossible because it was within range of the German guns now outside the town. Some of the ships were driven back to Dover, fearful of moving off the designated route that had been swept of mines. But the alternative was a very circuitous route avoiding the minefields, which took the ships far out to the east, before doubling back to Dunkirk, and was twice as long.

While these preparations were going on, Gort travelled to meet Weygand near the frontline, and both were delayed. They missed each other, but Gort found himself face to face with Sir Roger Keyes, the hero of the Zeebrugge Raid in 1918, the Portsmouth MP who had played a key role in the ousting of Chamberlain from Downing Street, who was wearing the full uniform of an admiral of the fleet.

Keyes was not happy. He was a friend of Leopold, King of the Belgians and his job as British liaison to the Belgian court had done nothing to corrode his admiration for the Belgians, under intolerable military pressure. He was also aware that Gort was in the process of withdrawing to the north, leaving the Belgian army exposed.

"Do the Belgians really think us awful dirty dogs?" Gort asked Keyes. He made no reply.

By then, the military situation was in crisis. In the afternoon, the British and French garrison defending Calais finally ran out of ammunition and surrendered. The only part of the coast now open to the BEF was a ten-mile stretch from Dunkirk to the small Belgian resort of La Panne. It was little to aim for, if they had time. And time was now running out – Hitler had now waited long enough and the stop order had been rescinded. It was too late in the day to start the panzers again, and it was soon clear that the command structure of the German forces was now so complex that, before any serious advance could be made, there needed to be a reorganisation. That took much of the next 48 hours.

Ramsay's instructions for the formal start of Operation Dynamo had been crafted by the First Sea Lord, Dudley Pound:

"The military situation was thought to have deteriorated so rapidly that the Vice-Admiral was informed by the Admiralty that it was imperative for 'Dynamo' to be implemented with the greatest vigour, with a view to lifting up to 45,000 of the BEF within two days, at the end of which it was probable that evacuation would be terminated by enemy action."

It is worth noticing how desperate this was and how small the extent of their ambition at this stage. Rescuing 45,000 men would not have been insignificant, but there would soon be up to ten times that number on the beaches, and most of them might have to be left to their fate. It was a despairing moment. At the same time, Eden signalled Gort "to operate towards the coast in conjunction with the French and Belgian armies". Again, it was less than completely honest.

Major-General Andrew Thorne had arrived with his staff at Dunkirk earlier in the day to set up the defensive line, but found the French general Bertrand Fagalde had got their first and was already doing so. Together, they agreed a line using the canals, with the French troops to the west and the British to the east, setting up three evacuation points, at Malo-les-Bains on the eastern edge of Dunkirk, at Bray-Dunes Plage further to the east, and at La Panne just into Belgium.

While the first ships were arriving in Dunkirk, Churchill and the war cabinet were meeting for the third time that day, and his own struggle with his Foreign Secretary was now joined: they disagreed about whether Hitler's terms, offered through the Italians, would be outrageous or not. Churchill said they would be worthless. He didn't feel strong enough to oppose him outright, and tried to delay a decision until they knew what was happening in Dunkirk.

For these first hours of the evacuation, Ramsay's attention was focused on the ferries, which were capable of lifting large numbers of men. To support their commanding officers, Ramsay had insisted on a naval lieutenant-commander aboard each one, plus ten seasoned sailors able to handle ropes under fire.

The plan was for a ferry to be in position to load and leave every four hours. The first one, the modern ferry *Queen of the Channel*, arrived back in Dover with 1,300 men aboard, and Ramsay watched it come into harbour with a huge sense of relief. Soldiers reported later that, thanks to Ramsay's preparations, there was hot stew waiting for them on board the ferries, but there were not enough plates aboard to serve so many. They had therefore been served in cocktail glasses.

In London that evening, Captain O. M. Watts, proprietor of the School of Sailsmanship in Albemarle Street, heard through the grapevine about the desperate need to navigators and others who knew how to handle boats. He sent messages to all his pupils that there would be no classes the following week, and urged them to report instead to the navy's London headquarters, based at the Port of London Authority next to the Tower of London. As many as 73 of his 75 pupils did so and were allocated to ship's lifeboats, some of them still in their city suits and bowler hats.

At the same time, Hitler was rubber stamping the reversal of the halt order. It would take some time, perhaps even days, to filter through, but Guderian now had permission to gather his forces once more and advance. In London, Churchill had dinner late with Eden, General Hastings Ismay, Churchill's military assistant, and Ironside, the new commander of British forces at home.

He ate almost nothing, brooding about Calais. When he got up from the table, he said: "I feel physically sick."

Total evacuated this day: 4,237

Monday 27 May

First thing in the morning, Captain Bill Tennant was in Dover with twelve handpicked officers and 160 sailors, preparing to board the old destroyer *Wolfhound*, ready to take control of the beach operation. He must have read the bizarre accuracies in the press that morning: "Allied troops are this morning firmly holding the Channel ports of Calais, Dunkirk, Ostend and Zeebrugge," said the *Daily Herald*, wholly inaccurately.

He had been asked to see the Vice Chief of Naval Staff in London the previous day and told him to "get the BEF back". His last instructions, before Tennant left the room, was: "Get all the guns you can". That was optimistic, given that they were still expecting to rescue only 45,000 men before the panzers over-ran the beaches. Tennant and his team were given a small taste of what they were in for as they crossed the Channel at speed in the morning: they were attacked by dive-bombers every half hour all the way across.

From experience in Boulogne and Calais, Tennant had a good idea of the chaos he might encounter of an army – possibly even two armies – in full retreat. He and Ramsay hoped that the distinctive blue of a naval uniform would be able to assert some authority, when army officers and men were all dressed in khaki battledress. On the way across, his sailors were issued with revolvers, much to their surprise, and were told they were to shoot anyone who tried to jump the queues.

Tennant's officers were sceptical and told him he needed some additional nomenclature. They decided he should have the letters SNO, for 'Senior Naval Officer', on his white helmet. There was no paint available, so he cut out the letters from the silver paper from a cigarette packet, and stuck them on with the pea soup he had just been served for lunch.

"The sight of Dunkirk in the distance gave one a rather hollow feeling in the pit of the stomach," he wrote later, capturing something of the horror of the port in these days. "The boche had been going for it pretty hard and there was not a pane of glass left anywhere and most of it was still unswept up in the centre of the streets. There was also a certain number of unremoved dead lying about from the last air raid."

The next air raid took place soon after his arrival. It was immediately clear that the plan to keep a destroyer permanently offshore as a means of communicating with Ramsay was not going to be safe. It was not clear, otherwise, how it could be done. The French Admiral Abrial was in back his underground bunker in the port, but the British were supposed to be waiting for Churchill to square it with the French before anyone discussed the dreaded word 'evacuation'. In any case, Abrial was proving difficult to contact.

It was also clear to Tennant that the Luftwaffe was soon going to have destroyed the harbour and docks at Dunkirk. They had already sunk two French and one British coaster in the docks and killed a thousand civilians in the town. The RAF had done their best but had lost fourteen hurricanes and five spitfires in the battles over the harbour. The shore batteries had also now been captured and were shelling ships on their approach, sinking the motor vessel *Sequacity*. Tennant realised the docks were no longer viable and they would need to use the beaches instead. The trouble was, he was advised by the army that the panzers would only take 24-36 hours to arrive.

Churchill had seen the decrypts of Hitler's order to resume the advance and was now completely convinced that Gort was right. He had urged Reynaud, the French prime minister, to consider withdrawing to the coast – but there had still been no mention of evacuation. Churchill liked Ironside, but was nervous that he was too pro-French, so he had accepted his offer to shift to a new command the night before. Perhaps the bitter signal sent to troops in Calais had convinced him of defeatism lurking in the War Office. Ironside was replaced immediately by Sir John Dill, his deputy.

Dill was never destined to get on with Churchill, but he was not tarnished by his links to the old guard in the way that Ironside had been so unfairly. Churchill had clashed again with Halifax at the war cabinet meeting that morning. Churchill was still not bold enough to oppose the Italian peace idea completely, simply warning that it "would ruin the integrity of our fighting position in this country". Halifax had persuaded Reynaud to express some sympathy with the idea – though actually both men regarded it very differently.

Halifax was also now cross, feeling misrepresented, and tried to pin Churchill down: would he ever consider any peace proposals by anyone? When Churchill refused to be limited by this kind of question, Halifax hinted strongly that he might resign. After the meeting, he asked Churchill to walk in the garden with him. Neither ever revealed what was said, but Halifax did not resign.

Ramsay was feeling the pressure, and aware of the pressure those under his direct command were feeling too. Commodore Wilfred Gandell, just back from Calais, visited him in the Igloo. "I remember going to his office in the small hours," wrote Gandell later, "and found him immaculately dressed, cheerful and fully alive, though I understand he had been up all night. Although pallid and slight of frame, he appeared tireless."

It was at this point that the Admiralty sent the first emissary to Dover to see how Ramsay was getting on under intolerable strain. Vice-Admiral Sir James Somerville was one of the most popular commanders in the fleet. He had been put on the Retired List by the navy before the war, as Ramsay had, in his case because of ill-health. Despite this, he was to be one of its most high-profile wartime admirals (it was Somerville who bombarded the French fleet in Toulon the following month), though he remained officially too ill to serve until the end of the war. He had been operating as a liaison between the Admiralty and Churchill's Downing Street office.

When Somerville saw the strain on Ramsay, day and night, having already had to deal with evacuations in Rotterdam, Boulogne and Calais, he asked permission to stay on and support him. From now on, Somerville and his team took over from Ramsay and his team at 2.30am and took Operation Dynamo through until after breakfast, so that Ramsay's team could get the sleep they so badly needed.

The most important issue was now the question of how to embark the troops. As far as Ramsay knew, the harbour was unusable and the Mole was just a walkway over the breakwater, and ships could not dock against it. Given that, the only option remained the western beaches, but one destroyer captain complained that it had taken him twelve hours to load 600 men by ferrying them from the beach.

The beaches were proving problematic too. The surf was running too high for the small boats to come safely and easily onto the beach. And when they got in close enough, it was difficult to stop the troops just loading in until the boat sank. Then they had to be righted, baled out, and the engines dried out and started again, before the whole cycle went round again.

The Luftwaffe were also now aware of what was happening and the air attacks were increasing. It was going to be hard to bring the bigger ships in during daylight.

"Evacuation tomorrow night is problematical," signalled Tennant on his first night. If they could not bring the ferries in during the day, then they would have to concentrate on the beaches until it was dark. So Ramsay abandoned his plans to have a rota of small craft and sent them all over at once. It was going to be tough but it was now or never.

On Ramsay's advice, the Admiralty stepped up their search for small boats which could ferry men waiting on the beaches out to the ships. It was a matter of urgency, so the Admiralty signalled all the naval establishments in the south to tell them how many whalers and cutters, the kind of boat designed to carry sailors from their ships to the shore, they could send.

Riggs and the Ministry of Shipping suggested that the Admiralty start searching the boatyards of south east England. So it was that naval volunteer reserve (RNVR) officers were told that, in the morning, they would fan out across the harbours and marinas of southern England, seeking out unregistered boats.

During the following day they managed to identify forty of them, mainly motorboats and launches, plus Thames barges and lifeboats which were all given RNVR officers and volunteer crews and ordered to head to Sheerness.

Ramsay asked also for any available destroyers from the nearby commands, from the commanders-in-chief in Portsmouth and of Western Approaches in Liverpool. Increasingly aware of the potential dangers, he ordered a screen of MTBs and anti-submarine trawlers and minesweepers to take up their positions to the north of the beaches to guard against attacks from the sea, either by E-boats or submarines.

At the same time, the senior officer at Ramsgate, Captain William Phillimore, agreed to take responsibility for repairing and refuelling the small boats so that they did not need to clutter up the harbour at Dover. Ramsay sent Captain Eric Bush on the destroyer *Sabre* to manage the sea end of the operation. By the time darkness fell, Ramsay had three hospital ships and two destroyers in Dunkirk harbour, another twenty destroyers waiting offshore, with the other paddlesteamers, minesweepers and MTBs strung out along the coast as far as La Panne.

The little ships were still in trouble. Most of those which had set off under naval instructions had assumed they should go to Dover and, and once they had set out, the vast majority had no wireless communication and could not be called back. It caused confusion and delay. Those being towed in the heavy swell then found themselves going in the opposite direction to others. There were collisions and more were set adrift.

Meanwhile, the new destroyers *Javelin* and *Jaguar* were lying off Bray, to the east of Dunkirk, and using their own boats to ferry soldiers out. It was a slow business, especially with the constant bombing. But the ferries were now going in every two or three hours, staggered to avoid waiting offshore, though the ferry *Mona Isle* was damaged by shells fire from the shore, having taken fifteen hours to load 1,400 men. She limped into Dover.

Bombardment from the shore was getting sharper, so Ramsay had no choice but shift the preferred route permanently to the long one in daylight, which meant that an 80 mile trip became 172 miles, past Goodwin Sands – and through an area that had not yet been swept of mines. Ramsay ordered his minesweepers to move fast to sweep a new, shorter route.

By now, men who had joined the queues on the beach when Dynamo had begun, 36 hours before, were just coming to the head of the exhausting line, without food or water – and aware that, if they dropped out for any reason, even to take shelter from bombs, they would have to go back to the beginning.

Even so, Ramsay's rapidly changing plan was starting to bear fruit. Five ferries, which had set off from Dover before dark during this day, took off nearly 4,000 troops. His small fleet of 17 drifters also sailed for Malo Beach and took off another 2,000 using their dinghies. At 10pm that night, Tennant ordered the Medway ferry *Queen of the Channel*, the most modern of the 32 ferries which plied their trade to and from Dunkirk, to try going alongside the East Mole, the 4,000 foot breakwater, a wooden gangway on top of a pile of boulders. Using ladders and planks of wood, 600 soldiers were quickly aboard.

The scene was apocalyptic, with stuka diver-bombers screaming down, and the black smoke billowing from the bombed oil depot, and the constant shooting in the distance as the rearguard forming along the canal to the west of Dunkirk kept back Guderian's advance guard. There were also the now familiar scenes of drunken chaos in the town. But there was a glimmer of hope.

Towards the end of the evening, British soldiers had dragged a man to see Tennant, explaining that he was a spy who had tried to smuggle himself into Dunkirk, and should be shot. Tennant was soon clear that the man was exactly who he claimed to be, an RAF officer who had been shot down over German-held territory, had found a bike and had cycled to Dunkirk. On way, he said, he had heard a noise and hidden behind a hedge while the tanks went by. It was then that he realised the panzers were going the wrong way – for some reason, they were driving away from Dunkirk.

It was the first indication for Tennant that there might still be a lull in the German advance long enough to collect the bulk of the BEF after all. The problem was that the BEF had not yet reached Dunkirk in force, and it was the other flank protecting their retreat, the one looking east, that was now under threat. The Belgian army was now down to its last auxiliary troops, using First World War artillery from the training college. They told Gort at 10pm that they had agreed to an armistice with Germany, starting in just one hour. It left a 25 kilometre gap that would need to be filled to protect them against the other side of the advancing enemy army.

General Spears in Paris phoned Churchill late and warned him of the Belgian intention. It was a desperate moment, but this time it was the Nazis turn to be unrealistically optimistic. "Only a few fishing boats are coming across," said Goering that day. "I hope the Tommies know how to swim."

In Marylebone, George Orwell and his wife went to the pub to listen to the BBC news at 9pm. "The barmaid was not going to have turned it on if we had not asked her, and to all appearances, nobody listened."

Total evacuated this day: 5,718.

Tuesday 28 May

This was the day the nightmare really became real. In the early hours of the morning, Ramsay's most modern ferry, *Queen of the Channel*, had been bombed by a single German plane, which took her to the bottom, though most of her crew and the 900 troops aboard were rescued by the stores ship *Dorrien Rose*.

Even more significant was the Belgian ceasefire negotiated by King Leopold, aware that his troops could no longer hold out. The Belgian government disagreed and went into exile in London, leaving Leopold behind. Gort's right hand man, Alan Brooke, destined for a critical role in the war effort, was moved from organising the rearguard to filling the gap with the British Second Corps. Even so, the Belgian surrender left seven French divisions cut off in Lille, effectively behind enemy lines.

The newspaper columnist William Hickey said that he had overheard a conversation about Leopold in an expensive restaurant that day. "I'm terribly shocked about it," said one man. "He was at Eton!"

Aware of the whole new danger to the BEF, Churchill wrote a memo to his ministers:

"In these dark days, the prime minister would be grateful if all his colleagues in the government, as well as important officials, would maintain high morale in their circles; not minimising the gravity of events but showing confidence in our ability and inflexible resolve to continue the war till we have broken the will of the enemy to bring all Europe under his domination."

Churchill went later to the House of Commons where he warned them to "prepare for hard and heavy tidings". It was a terrifying phrase for those who knew that the vast bulk of the British army was now facing imminent capture or annihilation.

Churchill's own battle was also reaching a moment of crisis. For days now, he had been tiptoeing around the looming disagreement with his rival for the position of Prime Minister, his Foreign Secretary, Lord Halifax. Halifax was, with increasing exasperation, proposing a different way forward: that they should put out feelers to the Italian government to see what terms Germany might accept to end the war.

Halifax was representing the views, not just of the Foreign Office, but of intelligent and informed opinion who believed, and with some reason, that

Britain could not fight on without an army.

Churchill had wrong-footed Halifax so far, without opposing him directly, but he knew the moment would have to come – and he was still not secure enough in his position to survive a high-level resignation or two from the former appeasers. Today, he had decided to call in reinforcements. The day before he had suggested that, the issue before them was so momentous that it made sense to include the Liberal Party leader in their discussions – knowing that Archibald Sinclair was not just a friend and former comrade-in-arms from the Western Front, but a long-standing anti-appeaser.

But his masterstroke was to hold the 5pm war cabinet in his room in Parliament, instead of in Downing Street. The war cabinet were meeting two or three times a day during the crisis, but the full cabinet still only once a week. By holding the war cabinet in Parliament, Churchill had the excuse to talk first to the 25 ministers of the full cabinet. As he briefed them about the catastrophe that appeared to be overtaking the BEF, he said, as a casual throwaway line: "Of course, whatever happens at Dunkirk, we shall fight on."

It may be that Churchill had quietly prepared his ground, or had some reason to expect what would happen next, but he described it as if it had taken him by surprise:

"Quite a number seemed to jump up from the table and came running to my chair, shouting and patting me on the back. There is no doubt that had I at this juncture faltered at all in the leading of the nation I should have been hurled out of office. I was sure that every minister was ready to be killed quite soon, and have all his family and his possessions destroyed rather than give in ... there was a white glow, overpowering, sublime, which ran through our island from end to end."

Churchill was writing this after the war. He may really have felt the 'white glow', but it was not the whole truth. He was not sure he would prevail, either against Hitler or the old guard he believed had led the country to such a dangerous position. Either way, this spontaneous demonstration had the desired effect. Halifax was not then able to push ahead with his proposals, at least with the determination with which he had intended.

A Foreign Office memo proposing that the crown jewels and Coronation Chair should be sent abroad immediately was given to Churchill that day. Three days later, he rejected the idea. Even so, he was not out of the woods yet: Chamberlain's supporter Henry 'Chips' Channon confided in his diary that a plot to oust Halifax would have to be thwarted by "all the gentlemen of England". Churchill was very far from secure in his position.

The Anglo-French politics were also coming to a head. The French First Army's new commander Blanchard, Gort's senior officer, went directly to see his British ally at Gort's headquarters, aware that the British were moving north. It was precisely the embarrassing interview that Gort had been trying to avoid. Silently, Gort handed Blanchard a copy of a telegram setting out his orders, which made it clear that the British were not just withdrawing, they were actually embarking. Blanchard lost his temper.

Gort replied that he expected to save only a third of his army, but it was still worth the risk. Blanchard said the whole idea was impossible and he could not take that option for his own men. His temper had barely cooled when he asked Gort whether he would delay for 24 hours to give the French First Army the chance to withdraw safely.

It was an agonising conversation. Gort said he had no time to spare as it was. If he did delay, as asked, he would be unable to comply with his order to withdraw.

There was a stunned and embarrassing silence. "Will the British troops withdraw northwards this evening, whatever the situation of the French First Army?" asked Blanchard. Gort said nothing.

It was left to Pownall, Gort's chief of staff, to reply with a simple: "Yes".

There was nothing else to be said. Gort's staff were already organising the bridgehead. British troops were already busy blocking the roads behind them with abandoned lorries. On the beaches, the advance guard was already leaving and had been for nearly two days. And after the meeting, Gort now ordered a general withdrawal behind the defensible line of the canal around Dunkirk, from Gravelines, Bergues, Furnes and Nieuport.

Realising he had no choice, Blanchard ordered the French to follow, adding significantly "the bridgehead will be held with no thought of retreat." The French had not yet completely grasped that the British were planning to leave altogether.

The sacrifices that allowed the BEF to escape were already being made. But surrender was not easy either: it was today when soldiers of the Royal Artillery and the Warwickshire and Cheshire regiments, who had surrendered outside the village of Wormhout outside Dunkirk, were ushered into a barn by their captors and two grenades were thrown in. Lives were saved when two NCOs flung themselves on top of the grenades before the exploded. Only a handful escaped to tell the tale.

On the beaches, the men were now being taken off with increasing desperation, given that the Belgian front had now collapsed. The bombing was less intense in Dunkirk, thanks to the heavy cloud, but the troops on the beaches were getting increasingly bitter that they were hardly ever seeing the RAF. This was partly because they were usually inland, trying to intercept the Luftwaffe before they reached Dunkirk, but it was also true that the RAF had neither the modern planes nor the trained pilots to cover the beaches all the time. But they were able to comply with Ramsay's request to bomb the German batteries which were bombarding Dunkirk pier.

The smoke from the burning oil depot was also making visibility difficult and the bombers began to stay away. As darkness fell, the burning oil provided illumination for the waiting soldiers and the small boats operating without charts. "The sight at night was magnificent," wrote Tennant later. "The red blaze simply turned night into day."

Before bed that night, Churchill composed a telegram to Reynaud, satisfied that he had seen off

Halifax's challenge, that "without excluding an approach to Signor Mussolini at some time, we cannot feel that an approach that this would be the right moment." The die was cast.

Total evacuated this day: 18,527.

Wednesday 29 May

Ramsay stood at the window of his Igloo at dawn, worrying about his transport ships. He could still see the smoke on the horizon, but the first ferry of the night had been due at 3am and it was now six hours late. Was the evacuation still possible? He had no means of finding out.

Apart from the incessant worry, he had some reason for satisfaction. The Admiralty had just sent a signal to all their available destroyers that they were needed immediately in home waters. The troops taken off the previous day had increased to over 18,000, and the prize had been won by the Isle of Man ferry *Tynewald*, which had carried as many as 7,500 troops back to Dover. The message from the King to Gort had been copied to him and it certainly concentrated minds: "Our hearts are with every one of you and your magnificent troops in this hour of peril."

But Ramsay was also getting reports of one of the worst nights of disasters for the navy, after a series of calamities in the early hours of the morning.

In the middle of the night, the old destroyer

Wakeful was torpedoed by an E-boat, and was torn in half, killing all but one of the 640 troops picked up from Bray-Dunes. The destroyer *Grafton* and the minesweeper *Lydd* arrived an hour later to pick up survivors. One of them was the Wakeful's captain, Commander Ralph Fisher, who was then washed overboard, picked up by the converted naval drifter *Comfort*.

Comfort manoeuvred near *Grafton* so that Fisher could warn her by megaphone: "For goodness sake get moving – you'll be torpedoed if you lie stopped!" It was too late. Even then U62 was creeping up, fired a torpedo which blew off Grafton's stern and put Comfort's steering gear out so that she was locked in a circle. *Lydd* then mistook *Comfort* for another E-boat, fired on her and the ship disintegrated and Fisher found himself overboard a second time in the same night (he was later picked up by a Norwegian ship carrying French troops and taken to Dover). *Grafton* also later sank.

Evan as the Admiralty was recalling its destroyers to home waters, they were also becoming aware of the enormous risk to the destroyers they were sending, and – given that they might be facing invasion soon – it seemed insane to risk the newest ones. That risk was underlined by damage to the destroyers *Jaguar*, *Galant*, *Greyhound*, *Intrepid* and *Wolfhound*, mostly by bombs, and all on 29 May.

As if these setbacks were not enough, the Luftwaffe were back at first light. Today would be their busiest day, trying to fulfil Goering's orders to destroy the BEF from the air. Churchill later dismissed the bombing because the bombs were muffled by the sandy beaches. "The soldiers regarded the air attacks with contempt," he wrote later. "They crouched in the sand dunes with composure and growing hope. Before them lay the grey but not unfriendly sea. Beyond, the rescuing ships and – Home."

But this was an idealised view. The horrifying scream of the diver-bombers had been enough to drive some troops out of their minds. It is true that the effect on rocks would have been much more murderous, but being bombed every hour or so on the beaches was quite bad enough, especially having to witness your comrades being disembowelled and living with the horror of civilians being bombed on the road on the way there.

The incessant dive-bombing led to a growing clamour among the soldiers on the beach against the RAF. And when they came ashore at Dover, they flung insults at those they saw in RAF uniform. Their concern was echoed in more diplomatic language by Ramsay and the naval staff. "Rightly or wrongly, full air protection was expected," he wrote later, "but instead, for hours on end, the ships offshore were subjected to a murderous hail of bombs and machine gun bullets."

Even so, as it turned out, the home squadrons were overstretched, flying four missions a day and having some effect. Churchill himself was at pains to make sure the RAF letdown story didn't spread, though in fact the RAF was learning new tactics the hard way – their losses were considerably more than the losses they were inflicting.

At the same time, Churchill was also processing his own rhetoric to Reynaud and working out what might be necessary to strengthen French morale without actually keeping the BEF in France. He urged Ismay and Dill to share arrangements for evacuation with the French and to offer to do so as fast as they could, "so that no reproaches, or as few as possible, may arise."

He also wrote to General Spears in Paris with a message to pass on directly to Reynaud. He promised there would be a new BEF, including

Australians, Canadians and regular troops brought back from Palestine. "I send you this in all comradeship," he finished. "Do not hesitate to speak frankly to me."

But as Churchill was reaching out to the French prime minister, the news from the beaches was that there were fierce disputes between the British, French and Belgian soldiers waiting there. There were claims that the French were stealing the uniforms from dead British soldiers so they could join the queues for the boats. The British were also telling their allies that they should be staying to fight for their own country. It isn't hard to imagine how enraging this would be for the defeated Belgians and the battered French soldiers who were leaving their own families behind to face the unknown.

Meanwhile, Tennant and Ramsay were arguing about the beaches. It was so much more effective if they could load men from the Mole in the harbour, and Tennant was keen to direct all the men there now that the surf was making it difficult to get the small boats onto the beaches. But Ramsay was aware that the small ships and boats which had been gathering at Sheerness were now on the way. And he was adamant that they should carry on using the beaches. There were fewer men now on the Dunkirk beach and more at La Panne, which is where the small ships were redirected.

The small boats had now largely made it to their collection centre at Sheerness, and research had been extended to yachting centres on the Essex coast like Burnham-on-Crouch. Trawlers were being sent down from the fishing port of Grimsby, powerboats were being sent to Ramsgate, where Phillimore was gathering a team which could service and refuel them very quickly – 170 powerboats would be serviced and repaired over the next week.

Meanwhile, the civil servants at the Ministry of Shipping had slashed the usual red tape. Any small boats or steamers they could find were signed up. The Ministry of Transport agreed to pay all the crews and all the expenses, and for any stores the boat owners bought, and would compensate them without question for any damage. Some of those crews were reserve officers or amateurs called out from their beds. One MTB was commandeered by a young man in striped pyjamas.

One study (see Sinclair Mackay's book *Dunkirk* in the bibliography) quotes sixteen-year-old Reg Vine from Eel Pie Island on the Thames at Richmond. He had to get his father to sign the form giving him permission to go with one of their boats and he was handed a pistol by the sub-lieutenant. What's that for, he asked?

"You'll be surprised," said the young officer.

"I bloody was surprised," said Reg.

At the same time, aware that their own forces were also now stranded at Dunkirk, the French navy was gathering what warships they could spare, given that many of them had been ordered to the Mediterranean to deal with the emerging threat from Mussolini and the Italians. There were now 32 ships under Admiral Marcel Landriau at Cherbourg, and waiting for the order to join in.

Under the White Cliffs, and almost cut off from the changing mood of the British press (*Daily Mail* front page: "How the BEF was trapped!"), Ramsay had time to rechristen his whitewashed operations room the 'Dynamo Room', but his main concern was increasingly now the state of the harbour at Dunkirk, which had become so critical to the evacuation. Dead bodies and bits of uniform were snagging the propellers of ships as they went in. But what alternative was there? It was too dangerous to expose the flimsy ferries offshore for the length of time it would take to load them from the beaches.

Ironically, towards the end of the day, the

Luftwaffe switched their attention from the beaches to the harbour. It was a moment when Dunkirk harbour was packed with ships. The modern destroyer *Jaguar* was damaged by bombs, but managed to limp back to Dover under tow, but the destroyer *Grenade* was badly damaged in the harbour and began to sink, fires raging aboard. Commander Jack Clouston, the Canadian naval officer in charge of troops on the Mole, slipped the moorings so that she would not sink there. The ferry *Canterbury* was also hit but made it back to Dover with nearly 2,000 troops on board, too badly damaged to be sent out again.

This was the nightmare scenario. One ship sinking in the wrong place in the harbour could block it completely and prevent any more undamaged ships from getting in. On the other side of the Mole, the transport ship *Fenella* began to sink too. A trawler was sent in to try and drag *Grenade* out of the way before she sank, and her magazines exploded with a huge bang just inside the harbour with the loss of most of her crew and those troops on board. For a miraculous 35 minutes, the old destroyer *Verity* managed to avoid the bombs, before she was able to slip past the sinking *Grenade* and escape.

"Little information of these disasters filtered

through to Dover," wrote Ramsay later, and he continued to send his ferries from Dover refuelled and with more boxes of food ready for the soldiers. So by 6pm, the transport ship *King Orry* arrived in Dunkirk to find it full of burning and sinking ships in the harbour and nobody on the Mole. *King Orry* became a target the moment she arrived and the captain very

sensibly turned straight around and set out to sea, aware of the danger of blocking the harbour. Once outside, her steering gear was put out of action by dive bombers.

At 6.30pm, the paddlesteamer *Crested Eagle* was hit by bombs as she turned away from the Mole and set on fire. Her commander beached her and the badly burned survivors were rescued by minesweeper.

At 7pm, Ramsay received a message via the Admiralty that Dunkirk harbour was now blocked by damaged ships and that all evacuation must now happen from the beaches after all. Later that evening, Ramsay told the ships not to approach the harbour at all, but to stay off the eastern beaches. It was a strange reversal of a day, though in fact – and he did not know it – the Mole remained undamaged, if only they could get alongside it.

But worse was to come for Ramsay. The Admiralty, terrified at the loss of so many of their most modern destroyers in just one day, had decided they could no longer afford to lose more. Ramsay would be left with just fifteen elderly ones to take off the bulk of the BEF, if he could manage to. The new ones finished embarking their latest loads of troops and, in the early hours of the morning, *Icarus*, *Impulsive*, *Intrepid*, *Ivanhoe*, *Harvester*, *Havant* and *Javelin* sailed to Sheerness in accordance with Admiralty instructions. *Montrose* and *Mackay* also left to be repaired, having been damaged inside Dunkirk harbour.

Still Ramsay was implacable: "Evacuation of British troops to continue at maximum speed during the night," he signalled in the evening:

"If adequate supply of personnel vessels cannot be maintained to Dunkirk East Pier (the Mole), destroyers will be sent there as well. All other craft except hospital carriers to embark from beach which is extended from one mile east of Dunkirk to one mile east of La Panne. Whole length is divided into three equal parts referred to as La Panne, Bray, Malo, from East to West with a mile gap between each part. La Panne and Bray have troop concentration points each end and in middle, Malo at each end. These points should be tended by inshore craft. Pass the message by V/S to ships not equipped W/T as opportunity offers."

It was clear from these instructions, asking ships to pass on the information, that Ramsay's communications difficulties were becoming intolerable. He needed more eyes and ears off the coast of France. He therefore sent his deputy, Rear Admiral Frederic Wake-Walker, who set out from Dover in the destroyer *Esk* that evening to go aboard the minesweeper *Hebe*, to co-ordinate the ships once they had arrived. He

took another 80 seamen to boost the shore party and a set of badly needed working radio sets.

It was clear that the crisis point was approaching. In a few spare moments that evening, Ramsay wrote to his wife:

"Just a few lines. The tempo is frightful and ever increasing. You will know by now what my task is: the most colossal ever undertaken of its kind and in circumstances without precedent. Everyone is stretched to the limit, doing magnificently, but flesh and blood can't stand it much longer. Officers and men cannot continue at this pace, but all are doing their best. No-one can foresee what tomorrow will be like. Perhaps it's as well. But we must keep a brave heart and trust that we shall be able to stabilise and retain our position against what is to come."

Total evacuated this day: 50,331.

Thursday 30 May

All the British divisions, or the vast bulk of them, were now inside the perimeter being defended around the canals of Dunkirk, and half of the French First Army was there too, though the five French divisions had been cut off by the German advance west of Lille and were fighting on under the effective French commander General Jean-Baptiste Molinié, with their ammunition and food now running low.

A German press communiqué explained what was happening – it could no longer be a secret – and boasted that "the German air force has attacked these ships with devastating results". It was nothing short of the truth and to celebrate it, Hitler himself flew into Cambrai airport to speed the process of re-organising the command structure of his armies in France.

What Tennant and his team could see was that the impact on the men on the beaches was also pretty devastating. Soldiers in the last stages of exhaustion and dehydration would sometimes just shoot themselves or simply swim out to sea. There were fights and occasional riots. Some officers were being shot when they intervened, and there were at least 100,000 men still stranded on the beach.

In an effort to clear the backlog, one of Tennant's team, Commander Hector Richardson in charge of Bray beach, suggested using the abandoned three-ton trucks driven into the sea to form a pier at high tide. In the Dynamo Room, Ramsay presided over a team of just sixteen; he needed this kind of imaginative insight from the wider team outside.

One of the team was in charge of charts. The rest were involved in one way or another in directing the huge fleet that had gathered under this direction, including 230 trawlers and small ships, 216 merchant vessels, four Dutch *schuyts* and about 139 other vessels of one kind or another. It was in its way the biggest armada ever pulled together, even if it was a motley one begged, borrowed or stolen for the event. Inside the tunnel next to the Dynamo Room were beds filled with sleeping men and women off their shift. There was support and understanding: one of the women telephone operators was kept in the dark about the sinking of her husband's ship, until he burst in to see her wearing a borrowed French uniform.

Beyond the Dynamo Room, Ramsay was also co-ordinating a much wider team – those at the Admiralty responsible for repairing the ships at high speed (125 repair vessels had been gathered nearby), at the Ministry of Shipping, in charge of supplying the ships; at the Shipping Federation where they estimated the minimum crew required to man a ship and were able to find them and send them to London, and then to Dover by car because the trains were all full of returning soldiers. Or Vice-Admiral Sir Lionel Preston at the Admiralty in charge of provisioning the ships.

Disembarking the troops at Dover was the responsibility of Commander Edward Jukes-Hughes, and the Ministry of Transport was in charge of organising 186 trains and their crews making nearly 600 journeys to take them on to London and beyond, with train drivers and firemen sent down from all over the country to drive them.

There were also elaborate and semi-voluntary arrangements put in place to feed the soldiers on the move, which meant catering available for loading onto the ships on the way out – while they were being refuelled and rearmed. It meant meals in tins handed to the soldiers through the train windows at places like Paddock Wood or

Headcorn, which they were then instructed to throw out of the windows as the train moved out, ready to be collected, washed and refilled for the next train.

But the day before had precipitated a crisis. There were small boats heading for Dunkirk in great numbers, but it was agonisingly slow loading people from the beaches. Ramsay had only one advantage, now that it was obvious to the enemy – and their allies – what was going on. There was no need for secrecy any more: they could appeal for boats and crews openly on the BBC.

Among the small boats which answered the call was one owned by the comedian Tommy Trinder, which was in Shanklin on the Isle of Wight. The boat got as far as Shoreham-by-Sea where it was taken over by the navy.

Before dawn, Ramsay had sent the old destroyer *Vanquisher* to find out if it was possible to carry on using the harbour. As the light seeped into the sky, her signal was received saying that there were obstructions but that it would work. It was enough for Ramsey to order the ferries back in. Things were beginning to look up again – as long as they never again bunched ships in the harbour to provide the Luftwaffe with such a tempting target.

Only one ship would load at any one time. To reduce the time spent in harbour, Tennant asked the soldiers queuing along the Mole to run along it and onto the ships. It was a tall order for those who had nothing to eat or drink, sometimes for days. It was also now clear that the Dunkirk town waterworks had been destroyed, and Ramsay responded by sending over new consignments of water and food to the waiting soldiers.

Much more worrying was the state of the crews after four days continuous work, day and night, under the most enormous strain, not to mention the terrible casualties aboard the rescue ships. The commanding officer of the ferry *St Seriol* lost the use of his legs from exhaustion, but refused to leave the ship when it docked at Dover.

Officers' legs swelled so much they sometimes had to cut off their shoes. Engine room staff lost their hearing, helmsmen forgot the course and couldn't remember it. There seem to be a pattern that, often after four trips to Dunkirk, crews would just experience physical breakdowns. To make matters worse, the big store ship *Clan Macalister*, sent to Dunkirk filled with eight new landing craft, was sunk by dive bombers on the way over.

Also the panzers appeared to be on the move again. The three service chiefs met in the

Admiralty map room in London and agreed that Dunkirk would probably be overwhelmed by the Germans the following day and – aware of Churchill's assurances to Reynaud – emphasised the need to get more French troops away if at all possible, if necessary by giving them priority.

There was also the ticklish question about what to do about Gort, now with his headquarters staff at the Belgian royal lodge in La Panne. He had won the VC in the First World War – this was not a man who would run away when he was in command. If they were not careful, he would be forced to surrender to the Germans and that would be a humiliating loss, not to say a compromising one.

Churchill crafted a letter ordering him, when the bulk of the BEF had left, to hand over to a major-general to command the last stages of the evacuation. He must then embark along with his men.

It was not a letter that pleased Gort, though it was an important one and the Americans were to study it nearly18 months later, before they ordered General Douglas Macarthur to escape from the Japanese in the Philippines, but Gort agreed. He also appointed Major-General Harold Alexander, later one of the most famous solders of the war, to take over the final stages of the evacuation.

By the end of the day, the fifth day, there was a meeting of senior commanders at Dover, chaired by Ramsay, which decided that – by the end of the night – the BEF would have been evacuated, leaving a rearguard of 4,000 men, which they then planned to take the following night. It was a tentative plan and it was not to be.

Total evacuated this day: 53,227.

Friday 31 May

Early in the morning came the news that the five French divisions which had been cut off near Lille had finally run out of ammunition. For four days, General Molinié had held back seven German divisions, giving the troops at Dunkirk time to escape. Now they had to surrender and as many as 50,000 French soldiers, mainly from French North Africa, were allowed to march into captivity. They may have bought an extra four days for the evacuation of the 92,000 British and 156,000 French troops now defending the area inside the canals outside Calais.

At the same time, Churchill and his deputy Clement Attlee, plus Dill and Ismay, were flying to Paris to meet the French war council. Few of them were there: Reynaud, Pétain – in civilian clothes – Admiral François Darlan, navy commander-in-chief, and General Weygand.

The first item on the agenda was the failing Norwegian campaign, and the decision evacuation British and French troops from there as well, plus the Norwegian royal family. Nobody wanted to lose another king to the Nazis, as they had just done in Belgium – and the divisions over Belgium lay unaddressed between them in the war council: Churchill had been understanding in public about the Belgian capitulation, aware perhaps of some British responsibility for it; Reynaud had been bitter and furious.

Then discussion moved to the western front and the dangerous situation there. Churchill told the French leaders that they had evacuated 165,000 troops so far, and 15,000 of them had been French. Reynaud and his ministers were frankly astonished. They had not understood that was the purpose, had been paying attention elsewhere, and had dismissed the idea as impossible. Reynaud paid tribute to the navy and the RAF for what they had achieved, but there was still some discomfort. Why the difference in numbers?

Because the French troops had been given no orders to embark, often refusing to board ships without the rest of their battalion, said Churchill. Darlan composed a telegram there and then to French forces in the area, ordering them to hold the bridgehead and explaining that British troops should embark first.

Churchill then seized the opportunity to make a gesture to buttress the alliance. "No!" he said.

"*Bras dessus bras!*" The two nationalities would embark arm in arm, and the British would form the rearguard. There was agreement around the table.

But the British had another item they could not discuss openly. They wanted to make sure the French were not considering, would never consider, breaking their solemn undertaking not to make a separate peace. Churchill made some remarks designed to set out his understanding of that agreement, introducing the idea – if their nations were over-run – of carrying on the fight from America if necessary. The sombre acceptance of the possibility of defeat by Pétain made them nervous. He seemed to accept that they might need to accept an armistice.

General Edward Spears, the British liaison officer with the French military was there, and he intervened in reply.

"That would not only mean "I suppose you understand, M. le Maréchal, that that would mean blockade?"

That might be inevitable, said one of the ministers.

But not just blockade, said Spears, "but bombardment of all French ports in German hands."

It was brutal, and strange with hindsight to realise that the British indeed bombarded the French fleet in Toulon and Mers-el-Kebir in only a month's time. "I was glad to have this said," wrote Churchill later.

"Your ally now threatens us," Pétain told Reynaud later.

At the time, Churchill's plan was to open a second front immediately from St Nazaire. Planning was under way. But the immediate result of his conversation in Paris was that Operation Dynamo would have to continue. The French military authorities had abandoned their plan to cut their way through the German lines and that meant the French would have to be taken off too. There might be another 50,000 French troops who would need lifting from the Mole and the beaches.

"It was like being told to run a hundred yards at top speed, and then when you'd done that, find that you'd got to carry on at once and do a mile," wrote Ramsay.

He had also been doing his calculations. His remaining destroyers were taking about 17,000 every 24 hours, and the ferries taking another 9,500. The other ships and boats were managing 15,000 each day. This gave a total of about 43,000 per day, but it wasn't enough. His new instructions and the numbers now on the beaches suggested the needed to get at least 55,000 a day. He knew French ships were on their way to help, but not how many of them. He phoned the First Sea Lord, Dudley Pound, and set out the figures – he needed his modern destroyers back if he was going to manage. Somerville intervened as well.

By mid-afternoon, *Harvester*, *Havant*, *Ivanhoe*, *Impulsive*, *Icarus* and *Intrepid* had been ordered back to Dunkirk. The decision came as a huge relief. Meanwhile, the latest appeal for small boats which could operate under their own power was having an effect. By today, 400 of them had gathered and were being sent over the Channel, many of them crewed by the boats' amateur owners, equipped with some charts but not very many – Ramsay's collection of charts had long since run short. Other crews were moonlighting desk sailors, like Captain Richard Pim from the Admiralty map room, who absented himself together with a handful of colleagues and managed to get hold of a Dutch barge, which they sailed over and brought back 800 soldiers.

Now, the Ramsgate and Margate lifeboats joined in, and the London Fire Brigade barge, which managed to make three trips. At 1pm, this

next group of a hundred small ships, took
Ramsay's newly swept Route X at 6 knots in a
series of chains of twelve boats each, plus six tugs
from Tilbury Docks towing 46 lifeboats taken from
ocean liners.

Unfortunately for the smallest ships, the wind
changed direction as they set out, causing a swell
big enough to turn some of them over. The
German artillery was also now close enough to the
easiest route to Dunkirk to bombard them on their
approach. But there was no doubt that the weather
was also improving. Also the beaches at both ends
were now being bombarded from the land, and the
sea approaches to them, which was terrifying for
the civilian crews. Ramsay instructed a
minesweeper to arrest any small ships attempting
to return without soldiers.

The little ships were now forming a symbol of
the whole evacuation, much to the irritation of
some of the naval officers who were there, who
pointed out later that the bulk of the BEF was
taken from the Mole onto destroyers. Brave and
reckless as they were, and facing real dangers too,
they did not have to work up to their waists in the
sea while being dive-bombed day after day, as
Tennant's team were doing.

"The small craft about whom so many books

have been written," he wrote later, "whose one, two or three trips to the beaches sounded very romantic, though they did a wonderful job, never went through anything like the tests of the people I have mentioned above."

Tennant had found it hard to contact the French naval authorities, underground in Dunkirk. Now Admiral Abrial was in contact and he agreed to cancel his orders to destroy the port installations so that the British could also use it. But the French ships were also now in action: just after midnight, dive-bombers sank the French destroyer *Siroco* with 770 troops on board and badly damaged her sister ship *Cyclone*. Later in the day, the torpedo boat *Bouclier* took off General Blanchard and his staff.

Tennant also made direct contact with Gort, now in La Panne, by walking the fifteen miles by road. He described what he saw:

"The road and country each side was packed with British army formations, and stragglers, French army formations, and stragglers, some parts of the Belgian army, and stragglers, French refugees and Belgian refugees with all their belongings in small carts. At the side of the road, nearly the whole way, were thousands of army lorries of all shapes and sizes, just pushed into the canal on one side or the ditch on the other. On top of this, add constant dive-bombing and you get something of the picture."

There were now also worries about the security of La Panne, as the Germans approached ever nearer. By midnight, 5,000 troops were taken off and the rest were marched along the beaches the ten miles to Dunkirk, again without food or water. Gort himself was now preparing to leave, spending the evening after his headquarters was evacuated watching the evacuation from the deck of minesweeper *Hebe*.

The writer Vera Brittain went walking in Regent's Park that day and noticed what she called "the strange illusion of peace". "We feel as though we are watching the funeral of European civilisations, elegantly conducted," she wrote. "Just so the Roman Empire must have looked before the barbarians marched in."

But in Oxford the same evening, C. S. Lewis was summing up the peculiar shift in public mood in a letter to a friend: "Oddly enough, I notice that since things got really bad, everyone I meet is less dismayed." This somehow goes to the heart of the strange paradox of Dunkirk, even today.

Total evacuated this day: 64,141.

Saturday 1 June

It was the Glorious First of June, a potent day in the British naval calendar, after Sir John Jervis' victory over the French in 1794, and at last it dawned bright and warm and mild. The sea was perfectly flat. These were perfect evacuation conditions. At Waterloo, Charing Cross and Victoria stations, huge crowds turned out to watch the French and Belgian refugees arriving with their belongings and to cheer the soldiers.

Much against his will, in the early hours of the morning, Gort had also left La Panne on a naval powerboat. The future military strategist Alan Brooke, the architect of the withdrawal, was also taken off in the old destroyer *Worcester*. Alexander was the youngest major-general in the army and was now in command of the remaining troops, and he was an excellent choice. He was visible on the beaches, always immaculately dressed, an enduring symbol of dignity and courage.

The bombers had been active in the early hours of the morning, crippling the railway ferry *Prague*, which managed to limp into port but not before decanting her soldiers to two naval trawlers. It had been a difficult night. It was only now becoming clear that there were no troops left at La Panne. When he discovered this, Wake-Walker ordered all the ships westwards. Tennant requested hospital ships, but Ramsay reluctantly explained that the government was discouraging taking wounded soldiers, because stretchers took the space for up to seven able-bodied men. All they could do was take wounded people on with everyone else where it was possible to do so.

Goering had cut short his tour of Dutch cities to invigorate his Luftwaffe attacks, and it was also clear from first light that the air raids would be intense. Nor were the RAF hitting back decisively – they lost six hurricanes and ten spitfires that day. The first victim was the destroyer *Keith*, which capsized off Bray-Dunes with Wake-Walker on board. Next was the minesweeper *Skipjack*. In both cases, the crews were rescued, including Wake-Walker, but most of the soldiers sheltering below decks were killed. Both the destroyers *Basilisk* and *Havant* were hit and sunk and, by the afternoon, the French destroyer *Foudroyant* was bombed and sunk.

Then, in mid-afternoon, the ferry *Scotia* and the venerable paddle steamer *Brighton Queen* were both attacked and went down with 2,700 French troops on board.

Ramsay sent out his senior officers in fast motor boats to collect up the strays and bring them home – ready to prepare them for another night, ordering all the ships to be out of the area by sunrise. In Ramsgate, they were helping to prepare the next wave of little ships, including local lifeboats and a number of tugs. It was due to be the final night on the beaches.

The plan was for all minesweepers, paddle steamers, *schuyts* and little ships would go to the beaches. At the same time, seven ferries, eight destroyers, plus nine drifters and a fleet of power boats from Ramsgate would go into the harbour. The French ships would go to the outer harbour, and about a hundred small French fishing boats would go to the beach immediately to the east, on the sea front.

"Things are getting very hot for ships," signalled Tennant at 6pm. "Over 100 bombers on ships here since 0530, many casualties. Have directed that no ships sail during daylight. Evacuation by transports therefore ceases at 0300. If perimeter holds will complete evacuation to-morrow, Sunday night, including most French. General concurs."

Don't order a fixed time to end, signalled Dill from the War Office. There were too many uncertainties still for that. Even so, the evacuation was going well and Tennant signalled that they could probably finish the process, if they remained lucky, by midnight the following night. Then an immediate complication: the British rearguard could not get onto the Mole because of the French soldiers. They had been expected by 2.30am but were diverted to the beaches instead – and Ramsay knew that the ships had been given orders to leave at 3. The Admiralty signalled the destroyers to stay until 7, but – for the smaller ships – the communications difficulties would mean they were out of touch. As it was, there was now so much smoke that some of the smaller boats, including some of the minesweepers, could not find their way to Dunkirk at all.

The casualties remained alarming, but as many as 60,000 men were taken off during the night. "Thanks to the unremitting determination of naval vessels who all executed a succession of round trips, interrupted only by the necessary refuelling and who accounted for 70 per cent of this total," Ramsay told the Admiralty. "The majority of the surviving vessels had been operating ceaselessly for at least five days, and officers and men are approaching a condition of complete exhaustion."

It was now not the bombs but this exhaustion that most threatened the remaining operation. Nor was it just the crews that were exhausted. The Loyal regiment, caught in a bombardment as they held the line at the Bergues canal, arrived at the Mole just before 3am to see the last two destroyers of the night casting off, and were forced to dig in back in the dunes until the following night.

Total evacuated this day: 61,557.

Sunday 2 June

At dawn, there were still 4,000 British troops holding the line at the canals in the outskirts of Dunkirk, plus seven anti-aircraft and twelve anti-tank guns. There were also French troops with them.

The evacuation was suspended during the day because Ramsay and Tennant felt it was just too dangerous. But they were planning a huge operation at night, involving 44 British ships and tugs and another 40 French and Belgian ships too, in one last desperate attempt to take off the British rearguard and any remaining French troops, as soon as it was dark enough.

Troops were now pouring through the suburban commuter lines of Kent and Surrey, and – now that the nation was fully aware of the stakes – a number of freelance efforts were under way in places like Sevenoaks and Orpington. One woman set up a table on a platform with all the bread and cheese she had in house. The policeman on duty spent his time cutting it up into squares. A local publican bought his entire stock of beer in a washbasin.

The beaches had now shrunk down to just one and a half miles. There was still frustration with the French on the British side, partly because the French troops would only go aboard with the explicit agreement of their officers, and only as complete units, which often led to delays. It remained next to impossible to contact Abrial, still in his underground bunker.

To his own crews, Ramsay made the following message:

"The final evacuation is staged for tonight and the Nation looks to the Navy to see it through. I want every ship to report as soon as possible whether she is fit to meet the call which has been made on our courage and endurance."

So close to the end, and there was a tragedy as one of the heroes of the Mole operation, part of Tennant's team of beachmasters, was returning to Dunkirk on an RAF motor boat which was attacked by bombers. Commander Jack Clouston was in the water and told the other boat to leave to avoid suffering the same fate. His body was never recovered.

There was also now a determination to do something about the wounded. Tennant requested a hospital ship that morning, and by the afternoon two were heading across the Channel. The idea was that they might be able to send in hospital ships during the day, if they were emblazoned with red crosses. But how to let the other side know?

Tennant's solution was to send an uncoded message, knowing that the enemy would be listening in:

"Wounded situation acute and Hospital Ships should enter during day. Geneva Convention will be honourably observed it is felt and that the enemy will refrain from attacking."

It was worth trying, but it was not a success. The first hospital ship, *Worthing*, was bombed two thirds of the way across and had to go back to Dover for refuelling. The second, *Paris*, left at 5pm and was attacked at the same spot. At quarter to eight, an SOS signal was received from *Paris* and tugs were sent out from Dover to bring her in. She sank at midnight, ten miles off the French coast.

The *Paris* sailed just head of the armada for the night, with 13 ferries, two large store carriers, plus destroyers, paddle minesweepers, drifters, *schuyts*, tugs and this time also six French destroyers and 120 French fishing boats.

During the day, the bombers were back and the ferry *Royal Daffodil* was bombed near the North Goodwin Light Vessel and forced back to Ramsgate. Alexander was taken out to the destroyer *Venomous*. By 11pm, the old destroyer *Winchester* found just 152 British soldiers (King's Shropshire Light Infantry) and took them aboard. Half an hour later, Tennant made the signal: "BEF evacuated" (what he actually seems to have said was: "Operation Complete. Returning to Dover"). He and his shore party returned to England, he said, unshaven and "looking like tramps".

But it was still not over. Abrial, in his bunker, signalled that there were up to 40,000 French troops still to come, either waiting or on the rearguard organising counter-attacks against the Germans. There was still more to do.

Ironside, now shifted to command home defence in the event of invasion, confided in his diary: "I still cannot understand how it is that the Bosches have allowed us to get the BEF off in this way."

"The usual Sunday crowds drifting to and fro," wrote George Orwell in his diary that evening in his Marylebone flat, marvelling at the apparent unconcern around him. "Perambulators, cycling clubs, people exercising dogs, knots of young men loitering at street corners, with not an indication in any face or in anything that one can

overhear that they are likely to be invaded within a few weeks." Orwell's much-loved doctor brother-in-law had been killed on the beach, tending the wounded at Dunkirk

Total evacuated this day: 23,604.

Monday 3 June

Ramsay had been wrestling with his conscience about whether it was possible to send his men again for yet another night to finish the job, when they were almost blind with exhaustion. Would it be "beyond the limits of endurance," he asked himself? He decided there was no option, but he told the Admiralty that, if another night was required, they would need to find a fresh team of crews. In the event, only one ferry reported it could not go out again.

But General Fagalde still had 25,000 men manning the rearguard and maybe 20,000 others – there actually turned out to be up to 60,000 hiding in the ruins of Dunkirk. Expecting a new German offensive, Fagalde wrong-footed them with an attack of his own, supported by their last ten tanks.

Ramsay stuck to the plan: no lifting during the day and then a regular planned approach to the harbour and the other beaches so that there was a flow of ships, and not too much waiting. But when the ships arrived at the Mole after dark, there were hardly any troops. Where were they? It seemed likely that they were taking part in the counterattack on the canal line on the outskirts. This time, there were no bombers and very little bombardment.

Even so, during the night, up to 27,000 troops were taken off. In the early hours of the morning, Admiral Abrial left Dunkirk on the French VTB 25. They hit a wreck on the way out, lost a propeller and he had to be picked up by the British destroyer *Malcolm*. From there, he was taken to Dover for breakfast with Ramsay. General Fagalde was also taken off. "We step over three or four English corpses," wrote one of his staff, "and three or four holes caused by bombs and we queue up at the end ... The fishing boats arrive at 10.30pm."

After midnight, the new naval landing party called out along the beach and nobody came. The formal agreement with the French, and Operation Dynamo, was formally ended at 2.23am on 4 June.

By the early hours of the morning, the first German troops were in Dunkirk harbour. There were by then thousands more French troops on the Mole, some of whom got away in small boats almost under their noses.

The last ships to leave were the British destroyer *Express* just after 3.15 am and *Shikari* twenty minutes later, towing two blockships. She took off another 300 troops, including the rearguard commander, General Robert Barthélemy.

Ramsay ordered a final sweep by air and RAF rescue boats. They found 33 French soldiers in a stranded barge near the Goodwin Sands, with two British seamen. During the day, more than a thousand more stragglers arrived in French and Belgian trawlers. Then it was over.

Major-General Maurice Beaufrère surrendered in the Hotel de Ville to Lieutenant-General Friedrich-Carl Cranz. "Where are the English?" asked Cranz.

"Not here," replied Beaufrère. "They are in England."

In England, Ramsay went out that morning to the golf course at Sandwich and hit what he called later the best round of his life. "The relief is stupendous," he told his wife, but his luck was clearly still holding.

Total evacuated 3 June: 29,641.
Total evacuated 4 June: 27,689.

Aftermath

At midnight on 4 June, Hitler decreed that church bells should be rung across the Reich to celebrate what he called the "greatest battle in the history of the world".

It had been extraordinary, but those British troops who returned to Herbert Morrison's new posters with the slogan 'Go to it!', who had escaped imprisonment by a series of lucky chances, felt strangely different about it. It had been a defeat, of course – and a serious one – but somehow the British, aided and abetted by the American press, came to see it as some kind of magical and heroic deliverance.

The cost had been high for the navy: nine destroyers had been sunk and 28 badly damaged. Ten trawlers were at the bottom of the Channel, along with six ferries. All the equipment and most of the weapons of the BEF had been simply thrown away.

But 700 British and 200 French ships and boats had taken off 338,683 troops, who would go on to fight in North Africa, Italy, Burma and Normandy. The difficulty was that only three of the sixteen infantry divisions which the British army could muster after Dunkirk could be equipped, and the RAF had lost 177 planes over northern France – more than they had shot down – with only 331 left to defend the nation. Of the huge armada of ships, as many as 236 of them lay at the bottom of the English Channel. Many of them had never been designed for anything like what they endured.

It had been amazingly lucky but it had also been an extraordinary achievement for Ramsay. He was a meticulous planner who had not been given more than five days to plan, but the rough and ready shape he had organised had worked, right down to the issue of disembarkation at home ports. Any congestion would have been a disaster. That meant that teams in every port on the south coast had to work with the local and naval authorities to make it smooth.

Then there was the question of refuelling. Every ship needed to be refuelled at the same time as the exhausted soldiers came ashore, some needed coal of various kinds, some fuel oil, and some diesel. Most bigger ships needed new anti-aircraft ammunition. All needed to be available and ready and in the right places.

Then there had been the emergency repairs that

needed planning for, and 175 ships were repaired during the operation. The rail authorities laid on 670 extra trains. And every ship had to know precisely how many men they could take, and how to make the most efficient use of the space. Not to mention the water and food every ship must carry. Amidst the disarray, people recognised that Dunkirk had been a shining and unexpected success.

Worse, no kind of detailed timetable had been possible. Ramsay had been given only a few days to plan all this, since the first Admiralty meeting on May 21 when he agreed to work out the contingency. The meeting with the French was only three days later and then at three minutes to seven in the evening of 26 May, they began the operation. What had begun with the forlorn hope that 45,000 might be rescued ended with more than seven times that number on British soil. For all this, the main credit has to go to Ramsay.

One of the officers who served with him summed it up:

"He drives by personal leadership and example, never sparing himself, nut at the same time taking less out of himself than most, because of his level temper, which I have never seen ruffled. He has wonderful judgement and refuses to be swayed by higher influences. I remember so well how he was at times badgered from higher quarters to do this, that or the other, but feeling that he – the Man on the Spot – was right, how admirably he resisted all pressure to do something silly suggested by higher authority."

"We must be careful not to assign to this deliverance the attributes of a victory," Churchill warned the House of Commons on the morning of 4 June. "Wars are not won by evacuations." The speech ended with his great peroration about fighting them on the beaches, which came to symbolise a kind of British defiance which, if it had emerged at all, found no real voice before Dunkirk.

Yet there was a kind of victory inside the deliverance, which demands to be heard somehow. If it was there, it was a victory of the new regime over the old, of courage and fortitude over rigid and implacable ways of doing things, and of flexible organisation and willingness to take part. It was, in short, Ramsay's victory – and the government recognised it by giving him an immediate knighthood.

"Actually I feel an awful fraud," he told his wife, "as the success if the evacuation was brought about by the combined efforts of a great number of persons. So it is not expected that I would be blown out with self esteem or anything like that, but I console myself with the knowledge that, if things had not gone well, I alone would have borne the responsibility and the blame."

If it was a victory, it was one in the great tradition of the Battle of Waterloo, about which Wellington said it was a "damned close run thing". It involved extraordinary luck, perfect weather conditions and a little help from Hitler himself, with his stop order. It was also bloody, painful, exhausting and it sent many of those taking part completely insane. It was not the picnic outing that it is so often portrayed as. It was tragic and it should not have been necessary.

But somehow the mythmakers were at work already, and perhaps most of all was the playwright J. B. Priestley, who captured something of the Englishness of the whole thing, the unofficial, last minute, cobbled together nature of it, in his BBC broadcast on 5 June, describing Dunkirk as an English epic, "so typical, so absurd and yet so grand and so gallant that you hardly know whether to laugh or cry when you read about them". He meant the pleasure steamers, leaving behind the innocent world of pork pies and peppermint rock "to sail into the inferno, to defy bombs, shells, magnetic mines".

It was a little how the British thought of themselves, as amateur soldiers, seaman and airmen, or all the other activities of wartime, sailing thoughtlessly but bravely into war. It was the English respect for amateurism, for unofficial action, which seems to have woven the bloody beaches of Dunkirk into a myth. For the French it was, at worst, a betrayal; at best, a disappointment: most of the French troops evacuated were sent back to Cherbourg four or five days later.

It also marked a parting of the ways, for those taking part as well as the nation. Those who had become, often through no fault of their own, identified with the old regime were often sidelined. Gort was given no new military command, though he proved a heroic governor of besieged Malta. Ironside did not hold an official position after the end of the year. Halifax became an effective ambassador to Washington. The French, of course, were in for a torrid time: Reynaud would be arrested by Pétain and would spend the war in prison. Abrial surrendered

Cherbourg to the Germans only a few weeks later and was sentenced to ten years hard labour after the war for collaborating with the Vichy regime. Fagalde was taken prisoner a fortnight later, spent the war in a German prison and was wrongly convicted of collaboration as soon as he got home (though he was exonerated later).

Those who were regarded as having saved the day became the mainstay of the British war effort. Brooke and Alexander went on to play central military roles. Tennant was captain of the battlecruiser *Repulse* in 1941 when it was sunk by Japanese dive-bombers, but survived to take charge of the mulberry concrete harbours at D-Day.

As for Ramsay, he looked forward to a brilliant wartime career, including taking charge of the D-Day landings, but he was killed on 2 January 1945 in a plane crash on his way to Brussels to discuss the defence of Antwerp during the Battle of the Bulge. He did not live to see the honours heaped on him in a well-deserved retirement.

It also marked a turning point for the nation. On the face of it, the British went through the trauma of Dunkirk shaken but not stirred.

Billy Cotton was on the radio on 4 June and the *Times* was advertising an Ibsen play in English on

Italian radio, broadcast on long wave from Rome. Wellington and beaten Marlborough at cricket on June 3, and there was a full report in the papers the following day. The long-running musical *Me and My Girl* was still showing at the Victoria Palace Theatre (the Queen had gone twice). Celia Johnson was in Daphne du Maurier's *Rebecca* at the Queen's Theatre, the film *Gone with the Wind* was showing at the Empire Leicester Square and the new comedy review *Haw Haw!* – a reference to the Nazi broadcaster – was showing at the Holborn Empire.

Yet something had changed. The British had turned their back suddenly, and not entirely voluntarily, on the networks of alliances that held Europe together. It was their generation's enforced, sudden and very shocking Brexit – and it meant that a new policy, to defend the nation militarily with almost no resources, had to be cobbled together at breakneck speed. It involved ordinary people as well as trained professionals and it was deeply traumatic, for those involved in the Blitz or the children orphaned or sent away.

Over the weeks and months to come – when Dover became the most bombed town in the UK – the idea took root that they had been led to near catastrophe by an old guard who had dominated the nation between the wars and refused to recognise the truth. It was a radical spirit and, in its own way, Dunkirk forged a new nation. The writer Stephen Spender asked Orwell on 6 June why it was that, over the past ten years, they had found it easier to "predict events than, say, the cabinet".

They wondered why this had been? Was it because those who had led the country had their attentions elsewhere? Had they been the wrong class, or just too wealthy, to read the signs? It wasn't clear.

Looking back on that summer, Orwell wrote later: "The English revolution started several years ago and it began to gather momentum when the troops came back from Dunkirk. Like all else in England, it happens in a sleepy unwilling way, but it is happening."

It was happening. In fact, in one almighty conflagration, one life-threatening crisis over the past fortnight, it had already happened.

Acknowledgements and further reading

Reconstructing the exact timetable of the Dunkirk operation and those events which affected it was not quite as easy as one might expect, given the number of printed sources and documents available. I am grateful as always to the staff of the London Library, the National Archives and the Imperial War Museum, but if I have misinterpreted what I have learned, the mistakes are mine alone. I hope I have managed to stitch an accurate narrative together which goes to the heart of an extraordinary two weeks in history.

I have been particularly helped by some of the following books and publications. In particular, Ramsay's own report to the Admiralty can be read online at:

http://www.ibiblio.org/hyperwar/UN/UK/Londo nGazette/38017.pdf

If you want to follow some of the stories yourself, I would particularly recommend:

A. J. Barker (1977), *Dunkirk: The Great Escape*, London: J. M. Dent & Sons.

Winston Churchill (1949), *The Second World War Vol II, Their Finest Hour*, London: Cassell & Co.

Richard Collier (1961), *The Sands of Dunkirk*, New York: E. P. Dutton & Co.

Douglas Dildy (2010), *Dunkirk 1940: Operation Dynamo*, Oxford: Osprey.

David Divine (1959), *The Nine Days of Dunkirk*, New York: W. W. Norton.

Kenneth Edwards (1945), *Seven Sailors*, London: Collins.

Nicholas Harman (1980), *Dunkirk: The necessary myth*, London: Hodder and Stoughton

Liddell Hart (1973), *The Other Side of the Hill*, 2nd edition, London: Cassell & Co.

John Lukacs (1999), *Five Days in May: London 1940*, New Haven: Yale University Press.

Sinclair Mackay (2015), *Dunkirk: From Disaster to Deliverance: Testimonies of the last survivors*, London: Aurum.

George Orwell (2010), *Diaries*, Ed. Peter Davison, London: Penguin Classics.

Hugh Sebag-Montefiore (2004), *Dunkirk: Fight to the Last Man*, London: Viking Penguin.

David Woodward (1957), *Ramsay at War: The Fighting Life of Admiral Sir Bertram Ramsay*, London: W. Kimber.

Other books by the same author in Endeavour Press and The Real Press

Fiction
Leaves the World to Darkness
Regicide: Peter Abelard and the Great Jewel

Non-fiction
Toward the Setting Sun: Columbus, Cabot,
Vespucci and the Race for America
On the Eighth Day, God Created Allotments
The Age to Come
Unheard, Unseen: Submarine E14 and the
Dardanelles
Alan Turing: Unlocking the Enigma
Peace on Earth: The Christmas truce of 1914
Jerusalem: England's National Anthem
Rupert Brooke: England's Last Patriot
Operation Primrose: U110, the Bismarck and the
Enigma Code
Before Enigma:
Codebreakers of the First World War
Lost at Sea: The story of the USS Indianapolis

By the same author:

Operation Primrose: U110, the Bismarck and the Enigma Code...

It was Winston Churchill who coined the phrase 'the Battle of the Atlantic'. "Amid the torrent of violent events one anxiety reigned supreme," he wrote later. "Battles might be lost or won, enterprises might succeed or miscarry, territories might be gained or quitted, but dominating all our power to carry on the war, or even keep ourselves alive, lay our mastery of the ocean routes and the free approach an entry to our ports."

Even Churchill's rotund expressions and mastery of language fails to quite do justice to the reality in mid-Atlantic, as freighters, tankers and liners were sent to the bottom in fire and burning oil, protected by an exhausted and dwindling fleet of destroyers and escorts, while increasing proportions of our imports lay in the ocean depths, along with their crews. It was a story of grit, daring, and frustration on both sides, and of long, tiring nights on watch from the sea-swept bridge of a corvette or a damp, freezing conning tower.

Meanwhile, ten more ocean-going U-boats were completing every month by the end of 1940, and the British ports were filling slowly with damaged merchant vessels that could not be repaired. In desperation, at the start of 1941, Churchill wrote a memo to the First Lord of the Admiralty, A. V. Alexander, the minister responsible for the navy, warning that cargo ships arriving in the UK that month were half those which had arrived the same month in 1940.

"How willingly would I have exchanged a full-scale attempt at invasion for this shapeless, measureless peril, expressed in charts, curves and statistics," he wrote later.

This was the reality that lay behind the desperate efforts to crack the Nazi Enigma naval code. Bletchley Park, the top secret wartime cryptography establishment, had its own stresses – but all those involved in the struggle to crack naval Enigma knew the stakes.

The performance of Benedict Cumberbatch in *The Imitation Game*, and the fascination with the life and work – and the untimely death – of Alan

Turing, has tended to throw the spotlight onto the extraordinary and secret work by these Bletchley Park code breakers. The narrative has concentrated on how the Enigma codes were cracked, and due respect has been given to all those aspects of the puzzle that came together – from the original Polish pioneers who helped to find ways of reading the early versions of Enigma and passed on their insights, and their Enigma machine, to the British, to the teams working around the clock in an obscure country house in the middle of Bedfordshire, from Turing's leaps of imagination and the beginnings of computing, to the inspirational contributions made by his colleagues which made the various steps possible.

By far the toughest aspect of cracking Enigma involved the complexities of the naval code. The army and Luftwaffe versions of Enigma succumbed to the code breakers relatively early and signals were read with increasing ease. But the naval versions still held out, for reasons that will be made clear in this short book.

The purpose of it is to tell a small slice of the story – the capture of a naval Enigma machine from U110 and its immediate consequences – but also to tell the tale in the context of one of the most important months in the business of cracking the naval Engima code, May 1941. That month saw both the capture of U110, together with an intact coding machine, just a few days after the first breakthrough – the capture of the naval Enigma settings for June – followed by the crescendo of the Battle of the Atlantic only days later: the pursuit and sinking of the German battleship *Bismarck*.

But the book has a secondary purpose. That is to try and set the story of the Enigma code-breakers at Bletchley Park back into the context from which it has been wrenched, the huge operation around naval intelligence which embedded Bletchley and the code cracking enthusiasts in Hut 8 in a wider machine that tried to use what clues were available to protect convoys, and read the minds of the enemy.

And perhaps most of all, the purpose is to set this story in the most important context of all: the fact that German code breakers had – even before the outbreak of war – been able to crack the British naval code, and while Turing and his collaborators were wrestling with the sophisticated Enigma system, their opposite numbers at B-Dienst in Berlin (until heavy bombing drove them out to the small village of Eberswalde) were reading most of the signals between the British Admiralty and its ships and convoys at sea.

This is not to diminish the achievements of the Bletchley people, which led to a series of individual victories from the Battle of Matapan to the Battle of North Cape, when the battlecruiser *Scharnhorst* was sunk. Harry Hinsley, who worked there himself – and wrote the definitive study of British intelligence in the Second World War – argued that cracking Enigma brought the war to an end at least a year sooner, because the U-boat threat had been comprehensively defeated at the start of 1944, allowing the necessary troops and material to be brought across the Atlantic to make D-Day possible.

There is no doubt about the crucial role that Bletchley played in the victory over the Nazis, and especially over the U-boats. But it is important to balance what we know of the bursts of individual brilliance with the systems and community effort of naval intelligence as a whole, and as it actually was – a day by day, hour by hour struggle by two sets of intelligence machines and, in particular, two sets of brilliant code breakers.

Part of the purpose of this book is to draw together that struggle when it reached its height, during that crucial month of May 1941 – when the very survival of Britain hung in the balance – to work out why one side managed by the skin of their teeth to develop the advantages that they could use eventually to defeat the other on the high seas.

Read more: see Operation Primrose, available on Amazon...

Made in the USA
Middletown, DE
01 August 2017